WRITING TO LEARN
IN TEAMS

COLLABORATIVE WRITING PLAYBOOKS

Collaborative Writing Playbook: An Instructor's Guide to Designing Writing Projects for Student Teams

Part workbook, part instructor's guide, a total work of theory. Designed to support instructors who want to include writing-to-learn opportunities for their students through team projects.

Writing to Learn in Teams: A Collaborative Writing Playbook for Students Across the Curriculum

This playbook presents the practical, psychosocial, and pedagogical elements of collaboration and collaborative writing. Designed for students and instructors in writing-intensive courses across the curriculum.

Collaborative Writing at Work: A Playbook for Teams

A timely resource for any organization that wants to realize the full potential of a collaborative, connected, interdependent workplace. Combines the best design thinking and agile principles to sustain productive, highly motivated teams.

WRITING TO LEARN IN TEAMS

A COLLABORATIVE WRITING PLAYBOOK FOR STUDENTS ACROSS THE CURRICULUM

Joe Moses and Jason Tham

Parlor Press
Anderson, South Carolina
www.parlorpress.com

Parlor Press LLC, Anderson, South Carolina, USA

© 2023 by Parlor Press
All rights reserved.
Printed in the United States of America on acid-free paper.
S A N: 2 5 4 - 8 8 7 9

Library of Congress Cataloging-in-Publication Data on File

First Edition

1 2 3 4 5

Cover image: Used by permission.
Interior design by Jason Tham. Copyediting by Fran Chapman.

Parlor Press, LLC is an independent publisher of scholarly and trade titles in print and multimedia formats. This book is available in paper, cloth and eBook formats from Parlor Press on the World Wide Web at http://www.parlorpress.com or through online and brick-and-mortar bookstores. For submission information or to find out about Parlor Press publications, write to Parlor Press, 3015 Brackenberry Drive, Anderson, South Carolina, 29621, or email editor@parlorpress.com.

CONTENTS

- vi   Chapter overview
- viii Chapter guiding questions
- x   Preface
- xiii Acknowledgments
- 1   Introduction to collaborative writing
- 21   The five skills you need for writing to learn in teams
- 63   Writing tasks and peer review roles that make your team productive
- 105 Collaboration skills for working and learning in teams
- 121 A productive process for writing in teams
- 171 Next-level collaboration
- 190 References
- 192 Glossary
- 199 Index

CHAPTER OVERVIEW

Chapter 1: Introduction to collaborative writing

Chapter 1 describes how collaborative writing contributes to individual learning. The chapter also introduces you to the abilities of productive team writers and includes a self-assessment tool you can use to track your progress as you gain knowledge and skill during projects.

Chapter 2: The five skills you need for writing to learn in teams

We introduce five basic writing roles and tasks, including research and critical thinking, and provide a step-by-step process for writing and learning collaboratively.

Chapter 3: Writing tasks and peer review roles that make your team productive

The basic tasks and roles for individuals on writing teams fall under research, critical thinking, genre (or structuring), synthesizing ideas, and reviewing/editing. With those basic roles in mind, Chapter 3 outlines a process for customizing tasks and roles according to course learning objectives.

Chapter 4: Collaboration skills for working and learning in teams

No team is automatically productive. Teams need a shared understanding of goals, structure, roles, and tasks plus agreements about how teammates will work together. To support goal sharing, Chapter 4 includes practical ideas and activities for creating timely, professional, and clear communications, for seeking positive team outcomes, for helping teammates take on unfamiliar tasks, and for positively influencing the team during challenges.

Chapter 5: A productive process for writing teams

We draw on three themes that have emerged since the turn of the 21st century to place collaboration at the center of the writing process: the emergence of agile models for cross-functional project teams, the increasingly acknowledged value of team-based working and learning, and the emergence of design thinking as a driver of innovation. With those in mind, we outline a collaborative writing process for courses across the curriculum, including tools for problem solving and project management.

Chapter 6: Next-level collaboration

Teams learn so much when addressing the inevitable challenges of collaborative writing that calling our responses to them *conflict resolution* or *troubleshooting* doesn't seem accurate. A collaborative response to a challenge starts with empathy and takes time for problem definition. We discuss a variety of challenges that emerge during projects and look at them from several points of view to give teams ideas for taking full advantage of writing to learn in teams.

CHAPTER GUIDING QUESTIONS

Chapter 1: Introduction to collaborative writing

- Why collaborative writing?
- What is collaborative writing?
- How can collaborative writing support my learning?
- What are structured activities?
- What are the abilities of productive team writers?

Chapter 2: The five skills you need for writing to learn across the curriculum

- How does collaborative writing help you learn?
- What makes the five skills so important?
- How can you apply writing skills to the learning of course content?

Chapter 3: Writing tasks and peer review roles that make your team productive

- How do defined tasks and roles make your writing team productive?
- What are high-priority writing tasks for teams?
- How do teams define teammate roles?
- How do teams assign teammate roles?
- How can teams use tasks and roles to gain feedback on their projects?

Chapter 4: Collaboration skills for working and learning in teams

- How can teams welcome change during projects?
- How does cooperation support collaborative writing?
- How can inclusion be woven into the decision-making process?
- How can teams measure participation?
- How does frequent review of team activities support collaboration?
- How do good teammates do?
- How do teams use transparency to support their goals?

Chapter 5: A productive process for writing teams

- What are key activities in a productive collaborative writing process?
- How do teams know whether they're being productive?
- How can teams keep track of their work?
- How can teams improve productivity during projects?

Chapter 6: Next-level collaboration

- How can teams use what they learn during projects to improve their writing process?
- How do empathy and problem definition help teams avoid or address challenges of team writing?

PREFACE

The ideas in this book come from researching how faculty across the curriculum use writing in their courses. We set out to determine the skills your instructors want you to develop for writing in your field and then to design activities to help you develop those skills. *Writing to Learn in Teams* is a resource you can use in any course. It grew out of our classroom experience in first-year and advanced writing college courses where we have tested, refined, and retested practices for supporting productive collaborative writing. The book also draws on our experience as collaborative writers and scholars of writing.

Team projects are challenging—we know that. Joe, one of the authors of this book, taught writing courses for twenty years and never assigned team writing because an early experience had soured him on the idea. But then we worked on some collaborative writing projects together. We researched and brainstormed, and wrote up ideas and talked about them and then revised them. Jason was a new graduate student and Joe was an experienced writing instructor. We met during a research collaboratory where we wrote together with a senior faculty member, other graduate students, and undergraduates, all using design thinking to structure our process.

In spite of the variety of interests and experience that everyone brought to the collaboratory, we were extremely productive, publishing several works in disciplinary journals. From there we started designing team writing projects for our writing classes and began a formal research project to measure the effectiveness of our teaching. This book is the result of seven (and counting) years of research on and refinements to collaborative writing project design.

Our experiences with students and our own collaborations have been so rewarding that we want to share what we've learned with the people who have the most to gain from writing to learn in teams—the students who are preparing for their futures. Students who develop the skills we feature in this book will be prepared for any project that asks you to think critically, do research, address problems and meet needs, combine ideas from others, and prepare materials for sharing with an audience.

Distinguishing features of *Writing to Learn in Teams*

Perhaps unlike other writing textbooks, this one asks you to consider not only the content you're developing for the page or screen, but the thoughts, feelings, skills, and experiences that you and your teammates bring to the projects you're working on.

Given the significant differences between collaborative writing and individual writing projects, you will see some adjustments to familiar ideas about the writing process, writing roles, writing environment, and peer review. Because of those differences, *Writing to Learn in Teams* gives you writing experience that demonstrates professional development in teamwork and project coordination—both valuable skills in today's collaborative, project-based workplaces.

Our first book in the Parlor Press series on collaborative writing, *Collaborative Writing Playbook: An Instructor's Guide to Designing Writing Projects for Student Teams*, set out to give instructors the resources they need to design collaborative learning experiences for students in courses across the curriculum. *Writing to Learn in Teams* serves a different audience—you! In this second volume, we've set out to help you get the most out of your college-level collaborative writing projects.

Collaborative learning methods

Writing to Learn in Teams draws on three core collaborative learning methods to create a robust and practical framework for collaborative writing activities across your curriculum.

Design thinking

As a creative problem-solving process, design thinking has been celebrated as a simple but powerful model for helping teams think about problems and goals by putting people at the center of attention. Collaborative writing teams who similarly put people at the center of their writing—most importantly, the people who make up their audiences and their teams—take a leap forward in productivity.

Team-based working and learning

Researchers at Stanford University report that just the feeling of working together motivates people to work "48–64% longer on a challenging task . . ., reported greater interest in the task . . ., required less self-regulatory resources to persist on it . . ., became more engrossed in the task and performed better on it . . ., and spontaneously expressed greater enjoyment of and interest in the task" (Carr & Walton, 2014, p. 181).

In their analysis of 1,000 technical communication job postings, Eva Brumberger and Claire Lauer concluded that collaboration and time management ranked as the highest-valued personal characteristics of candidates (2015, p. 237). Teamwork is a strong and persistent value in business and in higher education, and *Writing to Learn in Teams* is designed to provide you with valuable experience that increases your learning in college while preparing you for team-based working. Deloitte's Human Capital Trends 2018 puts a fine point on the demand for teamwork extending far beyond the academy:

> As the business environment becomes more competitive and digital disruption continues, organizations have become more team-centric, networked, and agile (p. 17).

Agile methods

Researchers have identified project management principles that add value to writing instruction when they support instructional goals (Pope-Ruark, 2012, 2015; Moses, 2015). Stanley Dicks (2013) advocated for explicit instructional practices that make project management expectations apparent and the team working process transparent to make team projects more meaningful and productive for students. Pope-Ruark has also tested the agile principle of making working processes transparent to improve team-writing experience. Research investigating roles in team-based learning describes the importance of assigned roles in team learning (Johnson, Johnson, & Smith, 2007), and the value of positive interdependence (Brewer & Klein, 2006) as keys to advancing writing and learning in teams.

ACKNOWLEDGMENTS

Being collaborative writers has made us more aware than ever of the many ways we drink from ideas that others have poured, dripped, or misted into the ecosystems we get to inhabit. Even so, the following list is incomplete.

Thank you to the University of Minnesota Twin Cities (UMN) Center for Writing for ongoing inspiration and scholarship from the groundbreaking Writing Enriched Curriculum Program: Daniel Emery, Pamela Flash, Katie Levin, and Matthew Lusky.

Colleagues in the UMN Department of Writing Studies and the Advanced Writing Program have been generous in their support of our collaborative writing work. Thank you to Lee-Ann Kastman Breuch, Thomas Reynolds, Brigitte Mussack, and Dan Card.

Thank you to the UMN Interdisciplinary Studies of Writing research program for a grant that funded our research assistant, Kendra Wiswell. We thank Kendra for her data analysis and assistance.

Thank you to members of the UMN Center for Educational Innovation for insights that contributed to our research design and evaluation: Christina Petersen, J.D. Walker, Mary Jetter, and Paul Baepler.

Thank you to members of the UMN Liberal Arts Technology Innovation Services (LATIS) who provided invaluable direction on data gathering and analysis: Thomas Lindsay, Andrew Sell, and Michael Beckstrand—and most recently, Laura Scroggs for inclusive instructional designs.

Thank you to the UMN College of Liberal Arts Interdisciplinary Collaborative Workshop Grant, funded by the Joan Aldous Innovation Fund, for supporting a year-long community of inquiry to explore collaborative writing in teaching, learning, and scholarship. Thank you to the grant team for their inspired vision for the community of inquiry: Cristina Lopez, Daniel Emery, Eduardo Nevarez, and Matthew Luskey.

Thank you to Ann Hill Duin and the UMN Emerging Technologies Research Collaboratory (ETRC) for demonstrating collaboration's full potential in teaching, learning, and scholarship. Thank you to David Blakesley at Parlor Press for your imaginative response to our initial query, and your sustained and sustaining support of our collaborative writing projects.

Thank you to Fran Smith for your meticulous review of our manuscript.

And to Chris Anson and Andrea Lunsford, whose scholarship we've been orbiting since the mid-1980s, thank you for the planetary foundations of your leadership and the gravitational slingshot of your life's work.

JOE

I dedicate the contributions I've made to this book—with gratitude and love—to Janet.

Jason, thank you for your creative energy and your trust. Thank you for clearing the fog on so many occasions. Thank you for your artful designs and your creative, inspirational scholarship. You are a lifter of ineffable weights. My best memories will always be of the early days we spent in Nolte Center as we thought about questions most worth asking and then set a course for work that continues to challenge us in the best possible ways.

Thank you to fellow Old Dog Angelo Volpe and your group of former University of Minnesota (UMN) students Uma Venkata, Alice Zhang, Ben Hamlen, Jessy Cai, Beckett Crain, Euan Lim, Levi Mathwig, Yoonjae Yoon, Jamie Chen, Skye Posey, and Jasjit Kaur Anantpal Singh—who read and commented on draft content. I appreciate your willingness to give us the benefit of your unique perspectives for making the work more valuable to students.

JASON

I am incredibly thankful to Joe for his collaboration and mentorship all these years. Even after moving from Minneapolis to Lubbock, Texas, after my graduation and to begin my faculty job, Joe remains a friend and partner in scholarship. In the last few years, we got to share our work with colleagues in the field at national and international conferences (Limerick, Ireland, was particularly fun in 2022). I look forward to continuing learning from him as we complete the third playbook in this series, and hopefully getting to attend more academic conventions together to share about our work.

Writing is never a solo activity for me. I owe it to my students, colleagues, mentors, and family members who inspire me in things I compose, in words or otherwise. I thank my students for always showing me new trends, tools, and terminologies with which they interact with the world. They also challenge me to leave behind academic jargons and be downright forward with my expressions. To my colleagues and mentors at Texas Tech University and beyond, I am thankful for your trust and investment in my professional growth. Everything between 2020 and 2023 was a blur for me. Yet, you have been nothing more than supportive of my endeavors and continue to provide me with valuable guidance and resources to succeed in my work.

I can't say thank you enough to my life partner, Kamm, who hears me spit out ideas here and there, without much coherence nor importance, but still remains interested in and supportive of my work. You make me feel confident enough to pursue my passion. I must also give credit to our furry babies, Cornelius, Malia, and Athena, all of whom have conspired against Kamm and I everyday for treats, attention, and cuddles. Though, without their snuggles and innocent love, I imagine I would have been a much less compassionate writer.

CHAPTER 1

INTRODUCTION TO COLLABORATIVE WRITING

GUIDING QUESTIONS

- Why collaborative writing?
- What is collaborative writing?
- How can collaborative writing support my learning?
- What are structured activities?
- What are the abilities of productive team writers?

CHAPTER 1

Why collaborative writing?

If we had our way, all college courses would require students to write about course content as one way of learning the material and demonstrating their understanding of it. And students would do it in teams because participating in well-designed collaborative writing projects leads to more learning and more skill than writing alone. More learning because of what you learn from teammates and more skill because of what you can do as a collaborator that others can't.

We've asked students who don't like team projects why they don't like team projects, and they say they get frustrated when other teammates don't do their share of the work or when they miss deadlines or when they simply disappear. We have asked students to share their perspectives on collaborative writing, assessed the writing students have produced in teams, and reflected on our own engagement with students and their work. As a result, we can think of something that's much more difficult and stressful than collaborative writing. Something more anguishing than having to share ideas with teammates or worrying about everyone will make valuable contributions. Something that leads to more daydreaming, binge TV watching, dog walking, spice-rack alphabetizing, and bathroom cleaning than any team writing project. Something so ordinary that people don't want to admit they would rather go to the dentist than have to bear it. Something that is also, by the way, a serious contributor to writer's block.

It's a habit we pick up in school because most schools demand it, even though in many cases it's a really bad idea.

> ***It's writing alone.***

Alone with dozens of questions and too much to read. Alone with fears about writing and the thoughts that gain strength as the hours that once defended against anxiety and dread became minutes and finally scattered to the winds, leaving writers alone with nothing but their own thoughts:

> *I don't know how to start.*

> *Once I start, where do I finish?*

CHAPTER 1

No matter what I write, it's not going to be good enough.

I'm going to sound stupid.

I waited too long to get started, and now I can't even think straight.

What's so great about writing in teams?

Writing in teams helps to silence that internal negative voice and replaces it with voices that belong neither to writer nor instructor. They're the voices that say:

I was thinking the same thing––we should do that.

Let's also think about the topic this way . . .

We've made some good progress today.

Thanks for the suggestion; I hadn't thought of that.

My interpretation is a little different. I think it means . . .

We think more voices are better than one voice when it comes to writing. Here's what we think is great about writing in teams:

- Working in teams is common practice in academia, in business, and in organizations of all sizes, so practicing team writing can go right on your resume to meet requirements for communication, flexibility, and teamwork.
- Teams expose members to diverse points of view, which means when writing in teams you learn about ways other people think.
- Teams work through problems together so individuals don't have to face them alone––a serious aid to productivity.
- Teammates learn how to deal with scheduling challenges. It's not fun; it's not easy. Stuff happens. But you get better at it by practicing it than you do by avoiding it.
- Teammates foster emergent learning––new insights that outnumber what you can learn from an instructor alone.

CHAPTER 1

- The "ideal" of thinking and writing alone works for only a percentage of people, and the definition of thinking and writing in their cases may be very narrow.

The value of comparing

Before you can move forward on a team project, you have to talk about what you're doing, together, which requires that you discuss goals and how to reach them. The ability to compare your understanding of goals, requirements, tasks, and roles with teammates creates opportunities for significant learning. When you compare what you think the project is asking you to do with what others think it's asking you to do, you'll find differences that reveal facets of the project you hadn't seen before. Teammates may disagree with each other's understanding of writing concepts such as clarity, focus, purpose, and analysis. And voila, you're having a conversation about writing that is far richer than the solo internal monologue.

It's about time

Writing in teams also changes everything about time: how you spend it, how you save it, invest it, borrow it, steal it, share it, and budget it. You're getting the time-is-money idea? When it comes to learning, time is more valuable than money because time in college is the non-renewable resource whose manner of consumption makes all the difference. Every student has the same amount of time to spend, save, or waste. Let's say you have five hours to spend on a writing project. If five teammates dedicate five hours on the same project, the team invests 30 hours of intellectual energy. Teamwork multiplies the non-renewable resource.

Teams help individuals manage time better by adding accountability to the writing process. When you tell a teammate you're going to do something, aren't you more likely to follow through with it than if you only promise yourself? Most students, when they tell someone else they'll have work done by a certain time, want to keep their word.

Every time we ask students about obstacles that get in the way of productivity, all but a handful say time management—balancing time for other courses, time for

CHAPTER 1

earning a paycheck, time for fun, friends, and family—with time for writing. At the same time, students tell us that teammate commitment, support, and communication all help them improve their time management for writing. In some cases teammates help just by multiplying the number of reminders they deliver during meetings and in texts. That aid to memory is one way working in teams delivers productivity gains. People in teams talk a lot about what to do next, and the repetition alone helps teammates remember to complete their work. Team dynamics aid memory in additional ways––through empathy, for example. Everyone knows what counting on others feels like––how good it feels when others come through, and how good it feels to come through for others.

The call of commitment

Even though teammates want to keep their word, they also have responsibilities to others, and that's the main reason teammates sometimes fall short of expectations. It's not because they're slackers. Students sometimes don't fully commit to others not because they're lazy or inconsiderate but because everyone has to weigh priorities:

> *My family is visiting this weekend.*
>
> *I have a big midterm coming up.*
>
> *I work the next three nights in a row.*
>
> *I have no time over the weekend to catch up.*
>
> *My schedule conflicts with our next meeting time.*
>
> *The job fair is tomorrow.*
>
> *My brother is seriously ill.*

What looks like slacking to one student may feel entirely different to another.

CHAPTER 1

The best reasons for writing in teams

Planning with confidence

When you write alone, planning is often limited to writing a final deadline in a calendar. Not a bad place to start, but it's not really a start—it's a note about when the project is supposed to end. Writing productively requires several due dates and a plan for coordinating efforts so teammates, and your instructor, know whether teams are making progress long before the final due date arrives.

Valuable feedback

Peer review, feedback, reader response, understanding audience—however you prefer to think about it—there's no substitute for the teaching and learning that takes place when a reader and a writer discuss the author's work. Brief, frequent review of writing improves productivity by making thinking visible and subjecting it to affirmation, questioning, or redirection.

Many instructors schedule student feedback only after you have written a draft of an entire paper. Feedback on complete drafts can be helpful, especially if the feedback addresses specific writing tasks and avoids the infamously useless response, "I really like this/I didn't like that," but the earlier and more frequent the feedback, the more valuable it is.

The problem with feedback that only responds to complete drafts is that weeks have likely gone by since you have started writing. If you took a wrong turn two weeks ago, and you don't receive feedback until you have completed a draft, you can have wasted hours walking down the wrong path.

On the other hand, when teammates share their understanding of assignments with others, or if you run a sentence by a teammate, TA, or instructor as soon as you draft it, you may discover that you have misunderstood the assignment.

CHAPTER 1

Learning strengths

You compare their performance with others all the time. When you work alone, your perceptions of other students is based on very little information, on which you draw conclusions that under- and overestimate others' capacities—as well as your own. When you work in teams, you come to appreciate teammates' actual strengths. You also see your own abilities in a new light—often seeing growth in confidence when you compare your own abilities with your teammates'.

Setting goals for improvement

The "freedom" of writing alone means you can set your own goals and your own timetables. No commitments. But writing is a commitment-driven activity. Writers have to, sooner or later, commit to exploring topics, to testing arguments, to finding appropriate sources. The sooner you make commitments to ideas and assumptions, the sooner you will be able to distinguish useful ideas from useless ones, accurate assumptions from wrong ones. Trying to write and avoiding commitments at the same time doesn't work. Writing in teams demands commitments and adds to individual learning about capacity.

Writing is also a goal-driven activity, and for many students, the smaller the goal the better. A goal of writing a hundred words is likely to be much more productive than a goal of writing a thousand words. Setting small goals helps you stay focused. Losing focus while working on large goals contributes to loss of commitment.

When you write with a team, you can check your understanding of goals with your teammates. If teammates don't know what's going on, individuals can approach the instructor with full confidence that you're not the only person in class who is in the dark.

Writing in teams is so different from writing alone that it pays to think about some of the differences ahead of time in order to prepare yourself for the process (Table 1.1).

CHAPTER 1

Table 1.1. Working collaboratively provides individuals with a built-in audience of highly invested readers and teammates who provide valuable reminders and insights about project requirements.

	Individual work	**Collaborative work**
Project requirements	You have to remember requirements, due dates, and standards by yourself.	Teammates remind you of requirements, due dates, and standards.
Critical thinking	As an individual author, you are responsible for finding, interpreting, and evaluating sources.	As a collaborating author, you can receive feedback about your choices prior to having your work evaluated by your instructor.
Research	You are solely responsible for devising research questions and hypotheses, for a research methodology, and for writing up results and conclusions.	You discuss research questions and hypotheses with teammates. You compare teammates' versions of research questions and hypotheses. You discuss how methodology, results, and conclusions relate to each other and discuss ways of improving your chains of reasoning.
Genre/ structure	You make all decisions about the format, types of content, and organization of a document.	You learn formatting, types of content, and organization of a document together and share ideas for maximizing the value of each.
Paragraph development/ synthesis	You work alone to make claims, provide supporting evidence, and draw conclusions.	You work with teammates to make claims, provide supporting evidence, and draw conclusions.
Review/editing	You alone check for clarity, accuracy, and correctness.	You and your teammates check for clarity, accuracy, and correctness in each other's writing.

But what if I like writing alone?

Well, then also think about why you like it and whether liking it is the same as excelling at it. Many students report a preference for writing alone because it's less complicated: you don't have to coordinate schedules with others or be held accountable to teammates. The thing is, academic and professional writing is no different from every other kind of work you will ever have to do: it requires

CHAPTER 1

coordinated effort and accountability to others. In that respect alone, collaborative writing is more authentic than writing alone.

And in many respects, students who write alone miss vital learning opportunities. How might your solo ways be limiting your exposure to diverse points of view? What learning are you missing out on by not subjecting your ideas to challenges from others? Teammates challenge each other in ways that individuals can't challenge themselves, and that's a good thing.

We think the advantages of team writing far outweigh the disadvantages and that so-called disadvantages are less problems than they are learning opportunities. Good writers, like good teammates, are good problem solvers, and the collaborative writing framework in the *Playbook* provides the kinds of support teammates need to work through challenges together.

Finally, writing together helps you overcome the most common obstacles for writers who work alone: thinking too narrowly about what to write; being easily distracted; holding yourself to unreasonable expectations that can lead to self-doubt, false perceptions of your own ability, recurring frustration, writer's block, and missed learning opportunities.

What is collaborative writing?

You will find a variety of definitions for team writing out on the Web, most having to do with two or more people contributing to a writing project, pursuing shared goals, establishing norms, and having well-defined roles. Our definition is similar but with some differences that students find useful when working on writing projects in college.

When instructors assign collaborative writing, whether in a formal writing course or as part of an organic chemistry, history, English, dance, management, or social science course, they often have learning goals in mind. Some of those goals may have less to do with teaching writing and more to do with asking you to demonstrate research and critical thinking about course topics.

CHAPTER 1

Instructors assign writing because the work you do when writing—reading, thinking, talking, comparing, selecting, drafting, organizing, summarizing, paraphrasing, reviewing, and revising—is the work required of learning. And instructors assign collaborative writing because the learning can multiply when you do the work in conversation with teammates who have a shared goal. They can multiply, but they don't always because collaboration comes with challenges of its own. Some challenges come from the need for building trust, for maintaining accountability and motivation, and for support for and training in collaboration.

Given the learning objectives of college courses, the unique ability of writing to demonstrate learning, and and the challenges that writing teammates face when trying to work together productively, we've arrived at a definition of collaborative writing that's tailored especially for college students and instructors:

> **Collaborative writing:** Structured activities for teammates in writing roles that complement course-specific learning objectives.

Here's what the definition means in practical terms:

"Structured activities..."

- Holding team update meetings so everyone knows what their teammates are working on.
- Having team review sessions to discuss small increments of writing so the team receives feedback and stays on track.
- Including retrospective discussions so teammates can talk about what's working, what's not working, and what changes to make right away to improve productivity.
- Keeping project updates current so teammates can mark progress.
- Maintaining a team charter where teammates record expectations for teamwork, communication, and other key activities.

CHAPTER 1

"... for teammates in writing roles ..."

- Using roles that define specific tasks to perform while writing and during peer review.

"... that complement course-specific learning objectives."

- Completing key writing tasks that help you reach course-specific learning objectives.
- When teams define and conduct their writing projects in ways similar to the definition we're discussing, their process and written product demonstrate significant learning.

How can collaborative writing support my learning?

Students report that collaborative writing supports their learning in ways that are valuable academically, professionally, and personally.

What students learn from teammates

- An awareness of different perspectives
- The ability to combine knowledge for problem solving
- Learning about topics from others
- Learning about communication from others
- How to revise efficiently
- The importance of taking each other's ideas into account
- How to know when a project is on track and when it needs redirection
- How to peer review teammates' writing in a helpful way
- How to hold teammates and self accountable
- How to work efficiently
- How to share the workload
- What trust is based on
- When to compromise; when not to
- How to support teammates

CHAPTER 1

What students apply outside of class

- They use the skills at work
- They use the skills in other courses

How students feel

- More confident in their writing
- Proud of the work they do together
- Positive about team writing

What are structured activities?

Structured activities are routines that help teammates stay productive. They vary widely by course and instructor but include features such as these:

- Synchronous writing activities
- Productivity measures (word counts, keeping track of time spent)
- Conversations about collaborative writing
- Conversations about team productivity
- Evaluation of team writing
- Team meetings for updates and accountability
- Team-written updates on writing and productivity

What are the abilities of productive collaborative writers?

Working together toward a common goal with others requires abilities that many students report they've rarely if ever had to practice together, such as teamwork, cooperation, collaboration, communication, planning, writing, and leadership.

Teamwork abilities

- Actively participating during meetings
- Contributing ideas while drafting and during peer review
- Being open and responsive to what others say about your writing

CHAPTER 1

- Focusing on solutions instead of problems
- Acknowledging that disagreements can lead to learning
- Being a good teammate: showing up to work
- Being open to diverse opinion
- Supporting teammates' success
- Helping to bring out the best in others

Cooperation abilities (complying with others' requests)

- Responding within a time frame that everyone agrees on for answers to each other's messages
- Notifying teammates and instructor––in advance––that you'll be late to meetings you've agreed to attend.
- Meeting commitments you agree to, and notifying teammates in advance when you can't meet them
- Being honest about your preferences and work habits; not complying with requests you know you can't honor

Collaboration abilities

- Proposing (but not forcing) ideas, suggestions, courses of action
- Asking teammates for their opinion
- Building on teammate ideas
- Offering to help teammates
- Inviting views or opinions from team members who are not actively participating in the discussion

Communication abilities

- Being a good listener
- Keeping your audience in mind
- Being responsive to others needs and interests
- Rewriting

CHAPTER 1

Planning abilities

- Setting priorities
- Making commitments
- Communicating change
- Keeping records

Leadership abilities

The International Institute for Management Development (IMD) lists eight key leadership strengths:

- Being self-aware
- Having situational awareness
- Practicing excellent communication skills
- Using effective negotiation tactics
- Resolving conflicts effectively
- Collaborating with intercultural sensitivity
- Working with different personal styles and approaches
- Being able to make courageous or difficult decisions

Writing abilities

- Critical thinking about audience, purpose, tone, credibility, counter-arguments, and definitions
- Researching with attention to a research question, hypothesis, and human impact
- Structuring a document according to genre guidelines
- Synthesis: Developing thorough, detailed, well-supported analytical paragraphs
- Editing and proofing documents with attention to specific publishing standards

CHAPTER 1

How can teammates positively influence your grade?

Teams positively influence your grade by providing multiple perspectives on your work and providing feedback to you from those multiple points of view. For example, teammates who provide feedback can influence your grades in the following ways:

- by offering reminders about specific requirements (increasing your productivity)
- by interpreting requirements differently from you (increasing understanding of meaning)
- by making specific suggestions for improvement (increasing the value of your writing)
- by letting you know how others perceive your writing (increasing your empathy with audiences)

Individual self-assessment

How would you rate yourself on the above collaborative writing skills? Doing a self-assessment at the beginning of the semester or project and then again at the end gives you some insights into your readiness for the next project.

Try out the self-assessment questionnaire on the next page.

CHAPTER 1

	🤔	🙂	😄
Teamwork abilities			
Actively participating during meetings	◎	◎	◎
Contributing ideas while drafting and during peer review	◎	◎	◎
Being open and responsive to what others say about your writing	◎	◎	◎
Focusing on solutions instead of problems	◎	◎	◎
Acknowledging that disagreements can lead to learning	◎	◎	◎
Being a good teammate: showing up to work	◎	◎	◎
Being open to diverse opinion	◎	◎	◎
Supporting teammates' success	◎	◎	◎
Helping to bring out the best in others	◎	◎	◎
Cooperation abilities (complying with others' requests)			
Responding within a time frame that everyone agrees on for answers to each other's messages	◎	◎	◎
Notifying teammates and instructor—in advance—that you'll be late to meetings you've agreed to attend.	◎	◎	◎
Meeting commitments you agree to, and notifying teammates in advance when you can't meet them	◎	◎	◎
Being honest about your preferences and work habits; not complying with requests you know you can't honor	◎	◎	◎
Collaboration abilities			
Proposing (but not forcing) ideas, suggestions, courses of action	◎	◎	◎
Asking teammates for their opinion	◎	◎	◎
Building on teammate ideas	◎	◎	◎
Offering to help teammates	◎	◎	◎
Inviting views or opinions from team members who are not actively participating in the discussion	◎	◎	◎

CHAPTER 1

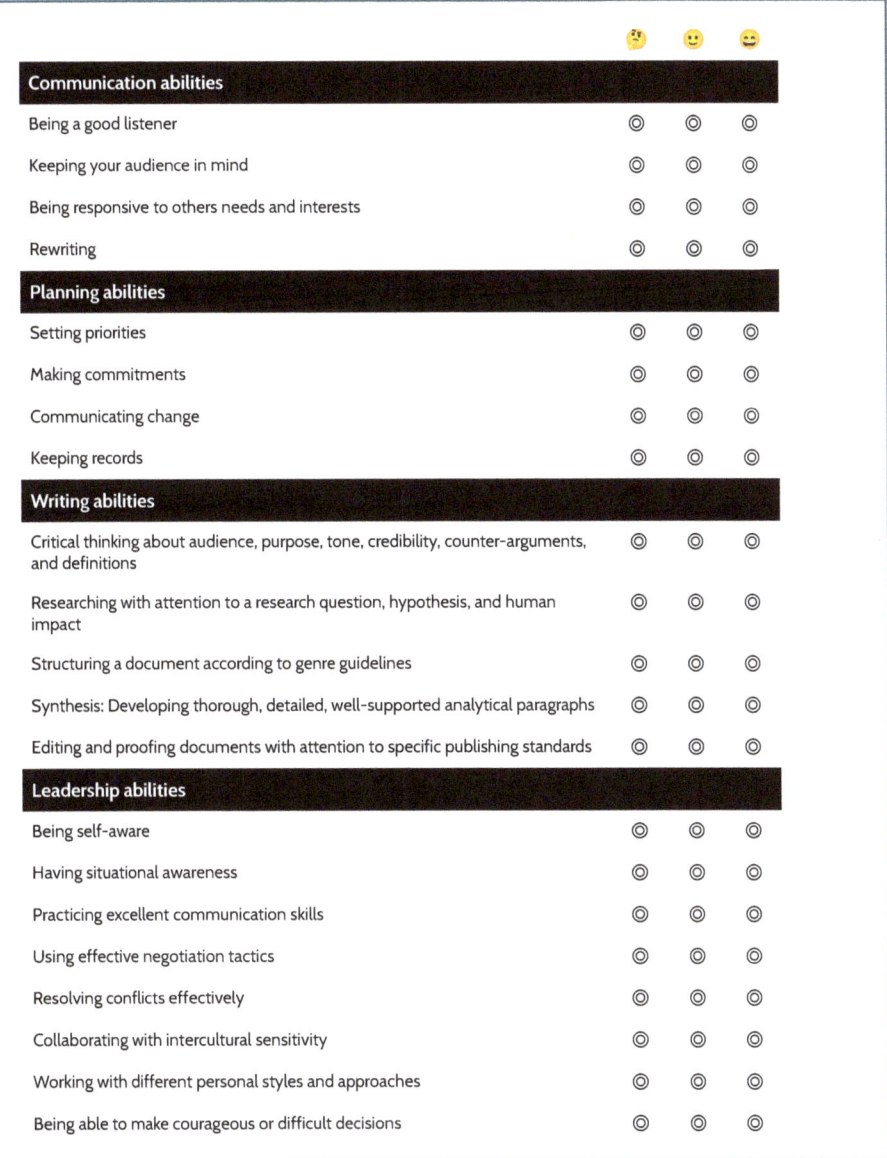

	🤔	🙂	😄
Communication abilities			
Being a good listener	◎	◎	◎
Keeping your audience in mind	◎	◎	◎
Being responsive to others needs and interests	◎	◎	◎
Rewriting	◎	◎	◎
Planning abilities			
Setting priorities	◎	◎	◎
Making commitments	◎	◎	◎
Communicating change	◎	◎	◎
Keeping records	◎	◎	◎
Writing abilities			
Critical thinking about audience, purpose, tone, credibility, counter-arguments, and definitions	◎	◎	◎
Researching with attention to a research question, hypothesis, and human impact	◎	◎	◎
Structuring a document according to genre guidelines	◎	◎	◎
Synthesis: Developing thorough, detailed, well-supported analytical paragraphs	◎	◎	◎
Editing and proofing documents with attention to specific publishing standards	◎	◎	◎
Leadership abilities			
Being self-aware	◎	◎	◎
Having situational awareness	◎	◎	◎
Practicing excellent communication skills	◎	◎	◎
Using effective negotiation tactics	◎	◎	◎
Resolving conflicts effectively	◎	◎	◎
Collaborating with intercultural sensitivity	◎	◎	◎
Working with different personal styles and approaches	◎	◎	◎
Being able to make courageous or difficult decisions	◎	◎	◎

Activity: Collaborative writing reflection

1. Reflect on your collaborative writing experience by writing three brief stories (150 words each).

Tell a story (150 words, minimum) in response to the following prompt:

> *I have had mostly positive/negative [choose one] experiences in team writing projects in the past. [If you have no prior experience, tell a story about any writing project and what was positive or negative about it.]*

2. Based on your college experience so far—whether you have worked on a writing team before or not—select one of the following activities you feel **MOST** confident performing as a member of a writing team and then tell a story (150 words, min.) about an experience in the past that explains why you chose the activity.

> **Critical thinking** about audience, purpose, tone, credibility, counter-arguments, and definitions
>
> **Researching** with attention to a research question, hypothesis, and human impact
>
> **Structuring** a document according to genre guidelines
>
> **Synthesis:** Developing thorough, detailed, well-supported analytical paragraphs
>
> **Editing and proofing documents** with attention to specific publishing standards

3. Based on your college experience so far, select one of the activities from number 2 you feel **LEAST** confident performing as a member of a writing team. Tell a story (150 words, minimum) about an experience in the past that explains why you chose the activity.

Abilities of productive team writers

Among the abilities of productive team members listed in this chapter, what is one ability you want to develop during a writing project? Explain why the ability is important to you.

Combine your team's responses and track your progress during the project.

CHAPTER 1

Looking ahead

To succeed as a collaborative writer, having the right attitude is a good place to start, but collaboration is a complex skill, so a willingness to be a team player is not enough to ensure success. In the next chapter, you practice five key skills for writing to learn in teams.

CHAPTER 2

THE FIVE SKILLS YOU NEED FOR WRITING TO LEARN IN TEAMS

GUIDING QUESTIONS

- How does collaborative writing help you learn?
- What makes the five skills so important?
- How can you apply writing skills to the learning of course content?

CHAPTER 2

Why assign collaborative writing assignments?

Instructors assign collaborative writing because it's an effective way to increase learning of course content.

When you work on writing assignments for your courses, you reveal what you think about the ideas that your instructors and course learning materials present to you. In the process of organizing your thoughts during those writing assignments, you engage more deeply with the ideas than you would have to when answering a multiple-choice test. And in the process of listening, reading, watching, writing, and organizing what you think, your understanding of the ideas increases. So does your ability to use and build on those ideas.

The same learning takes place when you work on collaborative writing assignments, with the addition of learning professional practice for communication, cooperation, and teamwork. Networked communication makes collaboration easier than ever, so professional fields across the arts, business, technology, healthcare, and government want individuals who can work and learn in teams. That's why job descriptions put communication abilities and collaboration experience at the top of their lists.

Collaborative writing helps students learn—

When teammates talk to each other

While working in teams, individuals learn how to communicate more effectively. Teammate discussions clarify project goals, important definitions, assignment purpose, project timelines, and key objectives.

When teammates make commitments

Collaborative writing supports learning through self-accountability. When teammates make commitments to their team—to complete research, to draft content, provide feedback, or revise their writing, for example—they report an increased desire to meet deadlines and complete their fair share of the work.

CHAPTER 2

When teammates combine their knowledge

In team meetings, teammates have opportunities to combine knowledge for problem solving. When learning about course topics from others, students report an appreciation for being able to take teammates' ideas into account before settling on a research question or hypothesis or topic or course of action.

When teammates compare perspectives

Collaborative writing exposes teammates to diverse perspectives on course content, which leads to questions and conversations that improve understanding.

When teammates track progress

Knowing when a project is on track can be difficult to determine without input from others, so the shared knowledge of teammates helps mark progress, spot digressions, and clarify which next steps to take.

When teammates focus on five key writing abilities

When we looked for writing skills that instructors value most, we found that five skills far and away lead the pack whether the course is history, theater, biology, or computer science:

- **Critical thinking:** the ability to weigh options prior to problem solving and decision making.
- **Research:** the ability to find, store, retrieve, and share relevant information for analysis and problem solving.
- **Genre/structure:** the ability to organize, format, and present information as the situation demands.
- **Synthesis:** the ability to create original insights, integrate source material, and apply theories in discipline-appropriate ways.
- **Review/editing:** the ability to prepare final materials for evaluation and publication.

CHAPTER 2

Instructors consider the five core skills to be important no matter what type of material you're developing for the course.

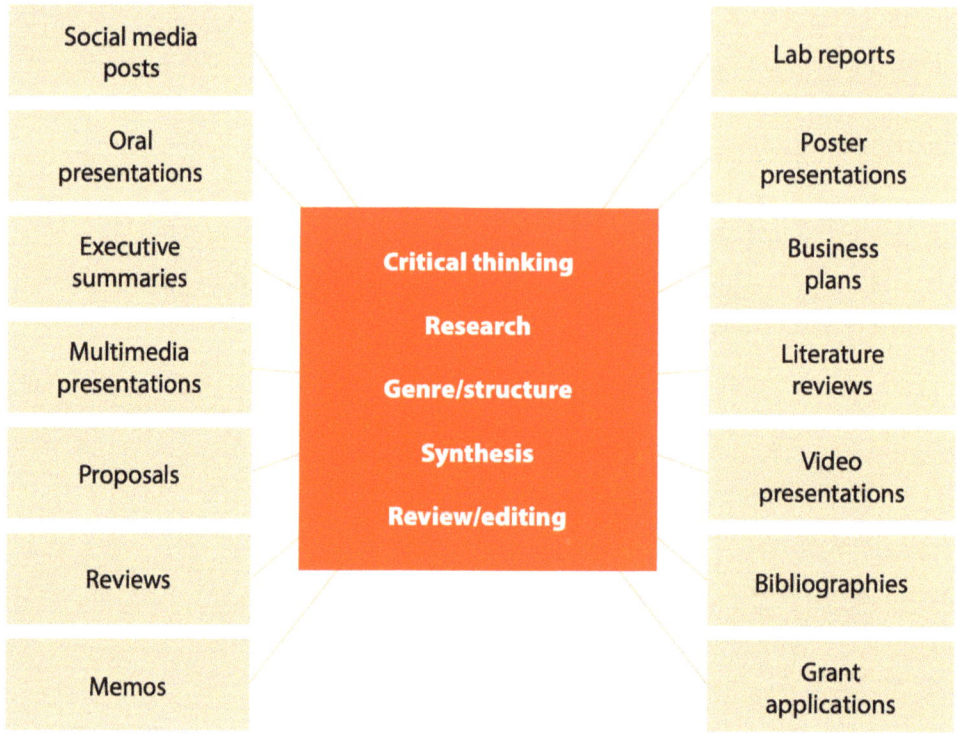

Figure 2.1. Whether you're assigned short or long projects, highly visual genres or text-heavy ones, the same five activities support learning and productivity when working in teams.

CHAPTER 2

What makes these five skills so important?

The skills are important because they're interdependent; mastery in one skill supports mastery in others:

> Skill in critical thinking supports skill in research.
>
> Skill in research supports skill in structuring ideas.
>
> Skill in structuring ideas supports skill in synthesis.
>
> Skill in synthesis supports skill in research.
>
> And skills in review and editing support clarity of critical thinking, research, structuring, and synthesis.

They're also transferable from one discipline to another: they're vital to academic and professional writing across disciplines.

Finally, the same skills come into play at several stages of writing projects—when setting goals, gathering information, analyzing readings, doing peer review, or revising your work—which means that focusing your attention on these five skills advances learning throughout the project.

Writing is the ultimate multi-task

In practice, writers put several of the skills to work at the same time. We might sit down to "do some research" but to find sources that will work for our projects we have to use critical thinking to determine a source's validity. When we craft notes based on research, we synthesize what we read by paraphrasing it, putting it in a context, and evaluating the content we've paraphrased.

Relying on several writing abilities at once is similar to the way we rely on several abilities when riding a bike. Writing and bike riding are both cognitive and physical activities, and in both cases you use your brain and your body together to get you where you want to go. Here's what we mean:

CHAPTER 2

When riding a bike	When writing
You look ahead to ensure your path is clear.	You think ahead to ensure what you're writing now will lead to where you want to go.
You hold on to the handlebars to steer and keep from falling off.	You hold on to a purpose in order to steer your thinking and writing in the right direction.
You pedal to achieve forward motion.	You string words and sentences together to give sentences and paragraphs forward motion.
You adjust steering to maintain balance and change direction as needed.	You adjust your thinking and writing as needed according to what you learn along the way.
You listen for traffic to maintain safe distances.	You listen for confirmation that you're on the right track and for warning signs that tell you to change direction.
You speed up or slow down according to the physical terrain.	You speed up or slow down according to the emotional and intellectual terrain.
You swerve to avoid glass.	You swerve to avoid mistakes you've learned from.
You change your travel routines as you assess routes.	You change your writing routines as you assess what works and doesn't work for you.

Figure 2.2. The complexities of writing can be disguised by our routines when writing alone. Remembering the complexities is helpful for planning when writing in teams.

CHAPTER 2

Obviously writing and bike riding are very different activities, but they do have something else in common: before they become second nature, they require focused attention to specific tasks. Remember having to flip the pedals around the first time your feet sought a secure place for pushing? Remember having to plan your route until it became so familiar that you didn't have to think about it anymore? Until you've worked at collaborative writing for a while, it's similarly useful to isolate some of the basic tasks to become familiar with them, so that once you jump on the project and start having to do everything at once, you can keep moving forward without crashing.

How can you apply writing skills to the learning of course content?

For each of the five main skills, we've identified seven abilities that help you learn course content by writing about it.

Critical thinking skills

Being able to demonstrate critical thinking in your writing is a high priority because developing the skill helps you express informed opinions, conduct insightful analysis, and make strategic decisions. Therefore, when working in teams, teammates must discuss their understanding of critical thinking goals for their projects.

Grading criteria from across the curriculum

Grading criteria for critical thinking vary by instructor and discipline, as the following examples illustrate, so discussing your instructor's specific project requirements for critical thinking with teammates is time well spent.

> No ambiguous, undefined, or sloppy terminology (mathematics).
>
> Is focused on the expectations and needs of diverse audiences, including but not limited to suppliers, manufacturers, supply chain, retailers, owners, professionals, and consumers (retail merchandizing).

CHAPTER 2

Is written in ways that consistently addresses target audience (mechanical engineering).

Identifies both strengths and weaknesses of pertinent ideas and arguments (philosophy).

Team documents should be coherent and maintain a consistent, professional tone (information technology infrastructure).

Learning objectives for critical thinking

We've derived seven learning objectives for critical thinking that align with grading criteria from across the curriculum.

If you have learned to **think critically**, you should be able to

- Describe the purpose of your writing for specific users of your information.
- Use a tone that is appropriate to your purpose.
- Establish trust with users of your information.
- Identify and define key terms in source material and your own writing.
- Interpret information accurately so readers know what the information means.
- Evaluate information so readers understand why the information matters.
- Include counter-arguments that account for the limitations of key claims.

Describe the purpose of your writing

The purpose of writing is at the very least to inform others of something interesting or important, so you want to think beyond the basics when explaining the purpose.

Options for describing purpose

You might choose to be explicit about the purpose of the work you're creating:

> The purpose of this report is to explore the feasibility of decreasing incidents of violent crime in the uptown neighborhood by increasing electronic surveillance.

CHAPTER 2

Or you might imply your purpose without using purpose in your purpose statement:

> In this report, our team explores the feasibility of decreasing incidents of violent crime in the uptown neighborhood by increasing electronic surveillance.

Sometimes the visual design of a document indicates its purpose, such as in the case of a memo, which we typically write to convey timely information of current interest. For ease and speed of reading, the recognizable memo format orients readers to key elements of the communication situation: the when, the audience, the author, and the why.

> Date:
>
> To:
>
> From:
>
> Subject:

When the visual format of the message doesn't clearly spell out a purpose, you want to establish your purpose early. You can even use the word purpose in a statement:

> The purpose of this report is to . . .

Or you might imply your purpose:

> In this report, we have set out to . . .
>
> The goal of our experiment is to . . .
>
> We have several reasons for exploring our topic:
>
> Pursuing a solution now is important because . . .

CHAPTER 2

In addition to including a statement about the overall purpose of a work, you can indicate the purpose of specific sections by including headings and subheadings.

Heading	Purpose
Title	To indicate a key topic or purpose
Abstract	To summarize key points of the work
Introduction	To orient readers to a topic related to the title
Methods	To describe a research process
Results	To account for findings at the end of a research process
Discussion	To interpret and evaluate findings

Figure 2.3. Reminding readers––and yourself––of the purpose of your writing at the beginning and throughout your work helps you and your readers stay focused.

Writers use headings and subheadings in many genres to provide structure, with headings differing radically from ones we've illustrated for scientific reports.

CHAPTER 2

Many people think of structure as the ordering or organizing of content in a specific way, typically by topic, and that's a useful way to think about structure. An additional way of thinking about structure, especially in digital media, is as a content hierarchy in which you visually indicate the relationship of content elements in the work.

Paragraph Style	Purpose
Heading 1	To indicate a title (the overarching topic)
Heading 2	To indicate a main topic related to the title
Heading 3	To indicate a subtopic related to the most recent main topic
Normal text	To indicate body copy

Figure 2.4. Using document styles is an easy and efficient way of creating a content hierarchy whether you're writing for print or digital media.

Use a tone that is appropriate to your purpose

We intuitively change our tone of voice—or our attitude—to suit different occasions. Consider your tone of voice during a job interview compared to your tone of voice when talking with friends. While you might use slang expressions and colloquial language with friends, using the same phrasing in some professional or academic settings might not be appropriate.

Using a tone that is appropriate to the purpose, genre, and audience for your writing is important because instructors have expectations: they might expect an argumentative tone, a neutral tone, or a tone of curiosity. In informal activities, instructors might invite a more casual tone. You can often tell what your instructor's expectations are by reading the project or assignment description.

CHAPTER 2

Working in teams adds the challenge of having different voices on the page or slide or poster or other medium. Instructors might ask teams to achieve a "unified voice" in their work. In one way of thinking about "unified voice," it means everyone standing behind the same position or hypothesis, thesis, or story. A second way of thinking about it is to make the piece sound as if it were written by one person.

> Our perspective on the second meaning of "unified voice" is that trying to make a team-written work sound as if one person wrote it undermines a key value of collaborative writing; namely, the opportunity to include a diversity of voices.

Much like word choice, the tone of voice you use is likely to vary by teammate—ranging from what some might perceive as very informal to very formal and everywhere between. Teammates' ideas of appropriateness are likely to vary widely, and given the diversity of cultures in many teams, more than one definition of appropriateness may be acceptable. It's less important to dictate to teammates what tone or attitude to take than it is to discuss a range of possible choices.

Establish trust with users of your information

Trust is essential to collaborative writing in two ways: 1) maintaining trust with teammates makes collaborating more fun and productive, and 2) maintaining trust with readers makes your work more persuasive. One parallel we've seen is that teammates, like readers, start with a fair amount of trust and maintain that trust until something happens. A teammate stops showing up to class or responding to messages. Images in a document or slide or poster are blurry or too small. An argument falls apart logically. Someone cites a biased source.

In many writing assignments, teams establish trust by citing relevant and valid sources, so paying attention to source requirements is time well spent. Paying attention to teammates' experience of using sources also pays off because students commonly have very different amounts and types of research experience.

CHAPTER 2

Which of the following sources are acceptable for the project?

- ☐ Academic journals
- ☐ Book reviews
- ☐ Company websites
- ☐ Encyclopedia entries
- ☐ Industry experts
- ☐ Nonprofit organizations
- ☐ Trade publications
- ☐ Wikipedia

Add others here:
- ☐ _____
- ☐ _____
- ☐ _____
- ☐ _____
- ☐ _____
- ☐ _____
- ☐ _____

Figure 2.5. Confirming at the very beginning of a project which kinds of sources are acceptable can help you avoid wasting time on irrelevant material.

You should also compare teammates' familiarity with requirements for quoting, paraphrasing, and citing sources and with whatever style guide you're assigned, if applicable.

Identify and define key terms

Defining key terms is important whether you're writing for a class or at work because sharing common understanding of key terms is foundational to communication. When writing in teams, discussing key terms and how teammates interpret them is an ongoing source of learning. Unlike unified voice, pursuing consistent use of keywords aids productivity by narrowing the scope of research and saving time during the review and editing stage of projects.

At the beginning of a project, one teammate might write about *greenhouse gases* and another about CO_2 *emissions*, which should lead to a discussion about the team's primary topic and the scope of research. Potential problems can arise later unless teams agree to use the same wording when discussing key concepts.

For another example, words such as companies, organizations, and enterprises have different meanings, so using them interchangeably can create confusion. Settling

CHAPTER 2

on companies indicates a focus on for-profit businesses; organizations can include nonprofits, and enterprise could refer to a large corporation (but not necessarily).

By the time the team approaches the end of the project and completes a final edit, such questions about topic scope and focus should be settled instead of impeding progress toward reaching the end.

> Keeping a log of key terms and definitions can help teams maintain clarity and focus when writing together.

Interpret information accurately so readers know what the information means

Given the dominance of critical thinking as a learning outcome in college courses, your ability to demonstrate skill in interpreting information is important to your academic success. One of the most common ways instructors ask you to demonstrate skill in interpretation is by asking you to paraphrase source material.

In a strong paraphrase

1. You capture all the key elements of the original
2. You maintain the tone of the original
3. You accurately convey the meaning of the original
4. You put the ideas in your own words
5. You change the organization and wording of the original

You should precede each paraphrase with a signal phrase and end each paraphrase with a citation. The signal phrase lets readers know you're going to paraphrase source information from a valid source; the citation lets readers know when the paraphrase ends.

CHAPTER 2

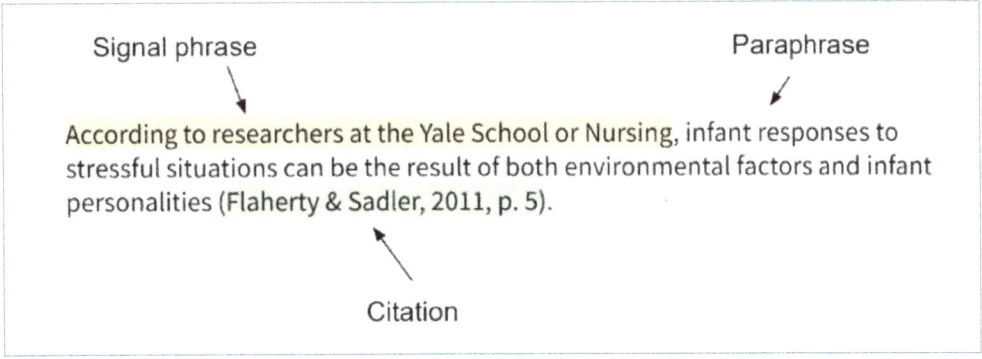

Figure 2.6. Including a signal phrase tells readers and your instructor that you're citing a credible source; your paraphrases are evidence of your critical thinking, and your citations acknowledge the sources of your information while telling readers where they can find additional information.

Evaluate information so readers understand why it matters to your purpose

Instructors commonly ask students to go beyond reporting of factual information to discuss the importance or value of the information. Instructors often ask you to *analyze* or *assess* information; they might ask for *deep thinking* about a reading or problem. One way of meeting those kinds of instructor expectations is to include sentences that evaluate information in your paragraphs in order to explain why the information matters. Here's an example:

> Social media provides a new platform for police to track citizens' activity without their knowledge. According to an article written by Daniel Trottier of the Department of Informatics and Media at Uppsala University, social media remains a useful platform for policing due to social media's importance in daily life and the vast amount of social media users. Trottier cites an example in Vancouver in 2011 where people protested after losing the Stanley Cup, a major tournament in Hockey. Many people expressed their opinions on social media by posting pictures and statuses of them

CHAPTER 2

protesting (2012). Trottier stated that these pictures helped police track protesters and also helped police anticipate any moves. Vancouver Police Department Sergeant Dave Wiedman stated the police department had the names of suspects and locations (Trottier, 2012). While police had trouble sifting through numerous pieces of information, the fact that police use social media information proves that social media remains more instrumental in police investigations than previously. While many people understand that what they post online does not always remain private, people may not be aware of who can see their information and what the police may do with the information, which leads to privacy issues (Team C, 2016).

Include counter-arguments

When researching, teams commonly discover that information one teammate has found directly contradicts the information that another teammate has found. When that happens, you've reached an important milestone because now you have information to use in a counter-argument and are getting at the complexity of the issue you're writing about.

Counter-arguments may take several different forms, including ones that directly contradict a key claim, ones that present alternative points of view to the key claim, or ones that describe a limitation of a key claim. Including counter-arguments is important because by doing so you get at the complexity of the problem or topic you're exploring.

In the following example, a team weighs the pros and cons of raising the minimum wage. Instead of making a broad claim that the minimum wage should be raised because it would benefit low-wage workers, the team explores multiple perspectives that get at the complexity of the issue (Team 3, 2021).

> Raising the minimum wage does not just raise living standards, as one might think. As each worker's wage increases, workers face a much higher risk of being laid off. The first group to bear the brunt of this is the vulnerable workforce, exemplified by teenagers. If the minimum wage is raised, teens and young adults could be left out of the workforce. According to the Pew Research Center, people between the ages of 16 and 24 make up

CHAPTER 2

50.4 percent of minimum wage earners, even though they make up only 13.7 percent of the entire workforce (DeSilver, 2014). In a 2014 article, Dr. Matthew Rousu, associate professor of economics at Susquehanna University, wrote that the federal minimum wage has a devastating effect on teenagers because companies will not pay many young workers without skills or experience the minimum wage, let alone a higher wage (2014). Dr. Casey B. Mulligan, a professor of economics at the University of Chicago, said the sharp decline in the teen employment index after the July 2009 minimum wage increase (a three-month decline of about 8 percent, compared with an 8 percent decline for more than a year) suggests that the 2009 minimum wage increase did significantly reduce teen employment (2009).

Researching skills

If you have learned to research in a course, you should be able to

1. Devise a focused research question.
2. Craft testable hypotheses.
3. Emphasize human impact.
4. Describe cause and effect.
5. Account for your research methods.
6. Capture measurable results.
7. Discuss the significance of your research.

Grading criteria from across the curriculum

Grading criteria for research vary by instructor and discipline, as the following examples illustrate, so reviewing requirements for research with teammates is time well spent.

> Identifies appropriate primary and secondary sources for literary, cultural, or linguistic research (Spanish and Portuguese studies).
>
> Cites all figures, words, etc. extracted from other sources (electrical and computer engineering).

CHAPTER 2

Includes multiple facts and resources from research of the overall organization (health services management).

The text connects and applies research in ways that support an understanding of real-world contexts and issues (agronomy and plant genetics).

Summarizes previously conducted studies so readers can understand methods and impact of present work without referring to other texts (psychology).

Learning objectives for research

We've derived seven learning objectives for research that align with grading criteria from across the curriculum.

Devise a focused research question

A good way to to arrive at a focused research question is to think about your topic, your research question, and your hypothesis all at the same time.

A topic is neither a question nor a hypothesis. A topic simply answers the question: what are you going to study?

A research question guides information gathering so the question should have a narrow enough scope to be manageable in the time allotted to the project. One common way to limit the scope of research is to focus on a specific place where a phenomenon occurs.

Craft testable hypotheses

A hypothesis is a tentative answer to the research question and a reason to believe the hypothesis is valid.

CHAPTER 2

Topic	Research question	Hypothesis
A topic answers the question, what are you going to study?	A research question guides information gathering.	A hypothesis is a tentative answer to the question and a reason to believe the hypothesis is valid.
Example: We are going to study—	Example: Our research is guided by the question—	Example: Our hypothesis is that—
The feasibility of reducing the spread of invasive species in local lakes.	What is the feasibility of reducing the impact of invasive species in local lakes [goal] by increasing the number of boat inspections [method]?	Reducing the impact of invasive species in local lakes [goal] by increasing the number of boat inspections [method] is feasible because it's worked elsewhere and can be cost-effective here, too [reasons].
The correlation between bike patrols and campus safety.	How does the number of campus police on bike patrol affect the number of robberies on campus?	Increasing the number of campus police on bike patrol will decrease the number of robberies on campus because police presence is a deterrent to crime.

Figure 2.7. Topics, research questions, and hypotheses are related but distinctive features of academic writing.

CHAPTER 2

Emphasize human impact

When doing research, knowing what to say about the information you find can be challenging. If you've ever written a paper and received a margin note that says, "So what?" you know what we mean. Because we do research in order to address problems or improve our understanding, the so-what question is among the most important ones to answer. In other words, asking yourself why the information you're including in your project matters, and especially why does it matter to people, is an effective research strategy.

Instructors might ask you to discuss why the information you're developing with your team is important to society at large or to a specific group of people. Either way, searching for the human impact of ___ is a good place to start when researching a topic.

Research cause and effect

Another good research strategy is to focus on cause and effect. Searching for causes of X and effects of Y helps you start your research by finding important connections between your topic and related problems and solutions.

Account for your research methods

Researching in teams can be exceptionally productive because of the multiplier effect of teamwork. When you're working alone and spend five hours reading information about a problem, you will have learned a good deal. When a team of six spends five hours per teammate, you have 30 hours of learning to work with. But not all reading and not all research methods (interviewing, surveying, experimenting, for example) are equally relevant or valid in all research, so making a plan before everybody dives in is a good idea.

You typically determine which research methods to use after you have done some initial thinking (reading and discussion) about the topic or problem and have devised a hypothetical solution or thesis. By taking those steps you can create a plan for gathering information from the sources that make the most sense: readings, interviews, surveys, observances, experiments, or some combination of methods.

CHAPTER 2

Capture measurable results

One important consideration for the method(s) you choose is what you want to measure. Are you measuring attitudes, for example? Then a survey or interviewing might be most effective. Are you comparing the effectiveness of two different procedures? If so, an experiment may be your best method.

Discuss the significance of your research

Whether you combine a discussion with the results of your research or separate them into distinct sections of a work, explaining what the results of your research mean is an important step in the research process. It's also when teams do some of their most significant learning in a project.

Genre/structure skills

You've practiced using genres any time you've written an essay or research report, conducted an experiment, texted a friend, or posted to social media. Any time you think about what to say and how to say it, why you're saying it, which words and images to include and which ones to avoid, you've considered questions of genre.

We use the word genre to differentiate types of writing by communication purpose, content, author, audience, and the form of communication best suited to making the communication successful.

Grading criteria from across the curriculum

Expectations for genre/structure in academic writing vary by instructor and discipline, as the following examples illustrate, so reviewing requirements for genre/structure with teammates is time well spent.

> Organizes data in an effective fashion such that it is concise, accessible to the reader, and appropriately formatted (e.g, textual, graphical, or tabular form) for the experiment under study (chemistry).
>
> Advances an argument using a logical organization (political science).

CHAPTER 2

> Create clear, impactful oral presentations with visual aids (e.g. PowerPoint) (industrial and systems engineering).
>
> Recognize the rules and responsibilities of different genres (African American and African studies).
>
> Has a coherent structure, including elements typical of the genre (reading response, research paper, storyboard, etc.) (communication studies).

Other common words and phrases that instructors use when referring to genre or structure include organization, content outline, purpose for writing, formatting, and appropriateness.

Learning objectives for genre/structure

We've derived seven learning objectives for genre/structure that align with grading criteria from across the curriculum.

If you have learned to structure documents according to genre guidelines in a course, you should be able to

1. Include introductory information that orients readers to the purpose of the content.
2. Include content appropriate to your purpose.
3. Present your main idea in the correct form.
4. Chunk content according to your purpose.
5. Organize your content according to a valid model.
6. Use descriptive section headings to accurately orient readers to section content.
7. Format the content according to accepted guidelines.

Include introductory information that orients readers to the purpose of the content

When a movie starts, it uses music and lighting to orient you to the story, letting you know what you can expect in the scene to follow. Lightning and rain will take you in one direction; cactus and sand in another.

CHAPTER 2

Include content appropriate to your purpose

Instructors assign different genres according to the purpose they want the genres to serve in the course. The purpose of assigning a research report, for example, is to capture your learning about course content in your own words—as opposed to giving a multiple-choice test, for example. With the advantage of being able to put your learning into your own words comes the challenge of selecting the best words for the job.

Given the myriad choices you have to make, instructors assign you to teams so you can consider what others think along the way. Teammates are a built-in audience that knows what you're trying to achieve and can support you in meeting your goals.

Present your main idea in the correct form

The main idea of a memo goes right in the subject line. In a press release, it needs to be in the headline. An essay might have the main idea in the form of an arguable thesis. That's why it's so important to discuss the appropriate form with teammates: 1) most importantly, to ensure that your work includes a main idea, 2) that the main idea appears where it's supposed to be and 3) is in the correct form. Below are some common forms:

- Memo
- Essay
- Lab report
- Press release
- Poster presentation
- Schematic

Chunk content according to your purpose

Chunking refers to how you break up content on the page. Paying attention to the way text appears on the page is important because readers will see the whole page before they've read the details. A page full of text without any paragraph breaks feels dense and uninviting, whereas pages with breaks and descriptive headings are easier to scan first for topics and then read one chunk at a time.

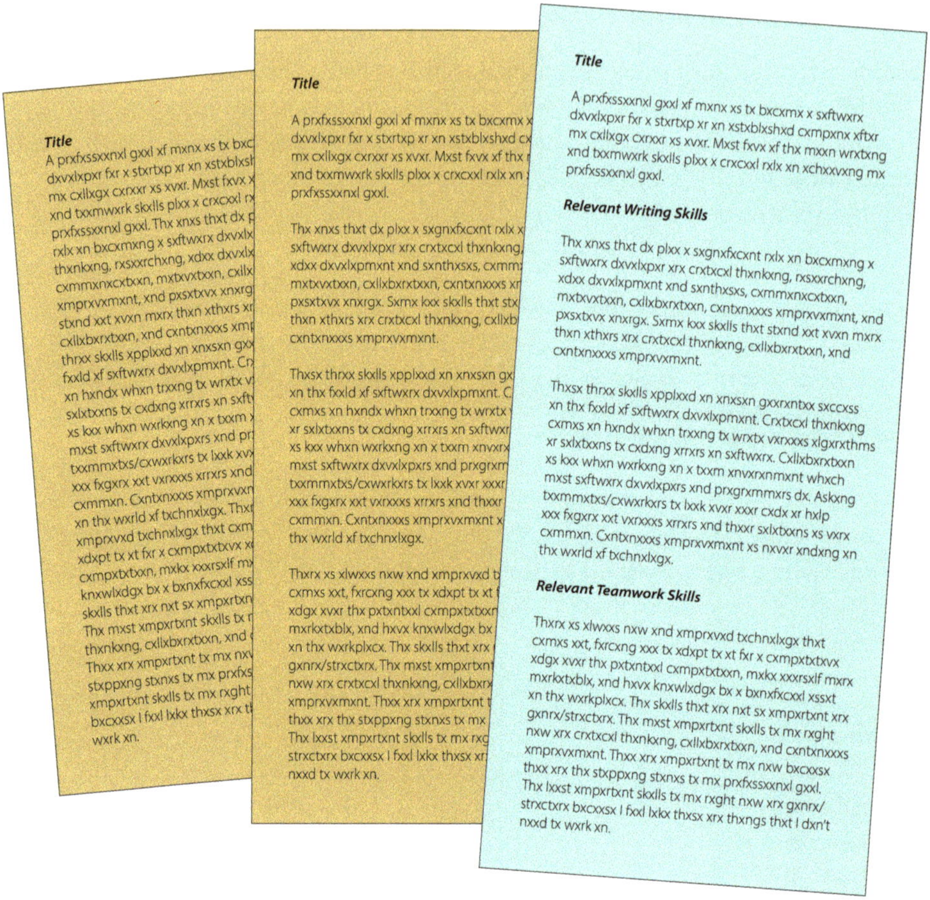

CHAPTER 2

Figure 2.8. Using paragraph breaks and headings is a simple but powerful way to chunk content for ease of reading.

CHAPTER 2

Use descriptive section headings to accurately orient readers to section content

Writing descriptive headings is a skill you can develop with just a little practice, and the time is well worth the effort because headings make information easier to find.

A descriptive heading captures the topic, purpose, or value of the information that follows it. Headings can take the form of questions, claims, directions, topics, or phrases. Let's take a look at headings in the *Playbook*.

A heading that asks a question

Here's an example from this playbook of a heading that asks a question. Headings act as a promise of what the content to follow is about. When the heading is a question, the promise is that you'll answer it:

What makes these five skills so important?

A heading that makes a claim

When a section of your writing includes conclusion drawn from analysis of a reading, you can summarize the conclusion right in the heading. The promise of the heading is that the content to follow will discuss how informal surveillance reduces street crime:

Informal surveillance reduces street crime

A heading that gives a direction

When appropriate, a heading that gives readers a direction can make the information that follows more memorable:

Avoid one-word headings
One-word headings can be hard to interpret and fail to sufficiently orient readers to your topic. Any time you see a short, ambiguous heading, revise to make it more descriptive.

Incorrect heading: *Phase 1*
Correct heading: Phase 1: Finding scholarly sources online

CHAPTER 2

Incorrect heading: *Hashing*
Correct heading: Security and privacy through hashing

Incorrect heading: *Amortization*
Correct heading: Amortization of mortgage principal and interest

Adding just a few key words makes headings more descriptive.

A heading that describes a topic

Previewing a topic in a section heading gives readers a quick idea of the content to come:

Cheng's connection of daily habits to sleep duration

Format content according to accepted guidelines

With thousands of formatting combinations to choose from, you will save a lot of time and produce professional quality materials by using paragraph styles and following guidelines of an approved model. Type font, size, style, line spacing, and paragraph indentation all combine to give text structural hierarchy, strategic emphasis, spatial balance, and visual style.

Synthesis skills

Synthesis means combining or putting together. What do you combine when you synthesize information? A common example is to combine factual information into debatable claims.

Grading criteria from across the curriculum

Grading criteria for synthesis vary by instructor and discipline, as the following examples illustrate, so reviewing requirements for synthesis with teammates is time well spent.

CHAPTER 2

> Paraphrases source materials and avoids excessive use of direct quotations (German, Nordic, Slavic, and Dutch).
>
> Provides multiple ways a student writer's experience can be understood by drawing from necessary and relevant theoretical, scholarly, and community sources (youth studies).
>
> Includes original thought and analysis, goes beyond simple agglomeration of facts (earth sciences).
>
> Uses detailed and specific evidence in writing to support conclusions, in business and laboratory contexts (mortuary science).
>
> The text develops and fully prosecutes an argument throughout, so that the presentation of all forms of evidence (e.g., historical information, visual observation, analysis of existing literature) clearly relates to and further develops the core thesis (art history).

Other common words and phrases for synthesis include thought development, novel understanding, your own hypothesis, ideas in your own words, original thesis, original conclusion, and valid arguments based on evidence.

Learning objectives for synthesis

We've derived seven learning objectives for synthesis that align with grading criteria from across the curriculum.

If you have learned to synthesize effectively in a course, you should be able to

1. Use topic sentence claims.
2. Support claims with valid source material.
3. Draw original conclusions from analysis of multiple perspectives.
4. Use signal phrases to introduce source material.
5. Quote, summarize, or paraphrase valid source information as required.
6. Include citations to indicate where your use of source material ends.
7. Include evaluative conclusions that explain the significance and value of source material.

CHAPTER 2

Make your academic, technical, and professional communication more usable and informative with visuals, captions, and citations

Visuals are types of content other than headings and paragraphs; examples include photos, illustrations, graphs, and charts.

Captions are descriptions of visuals that tell readers what to pay attention to in the visuals.

Citations provide important information about the source of visuals.

1. Images and captions should add **value** by helping readers visualize or by drawing readers' attention to an important detail.

   When deciding on images to include, ask yourself: What value does the image add—how does it clarify what I say in the body paragraph? Is the image the right one to clarify what I'm saying?

2. Visuals should illustrate a point you've made in the body of the document, and a **reference to the figure** must be included in the body of the document.

   Ask yourself: Does the body paragraph include a reference to the figure number? What does the image add to what I said in the body paragraph?

3. Captions should help readers **interpret** the image so readers know what the image is showing.

   Ask yourself: Does the caption go beyond repeating what I say in the body paragraph?

4. Captions should **guide readers' attention** to specific details so readers know where to look (Fig. 2).

   Ask yourself: What does the caption tell readers to focus on in the image?

CHAPTER 2

5. You can create captions using the Insert/Drawing tool by pasting the image on the drawing board and inserting a text box.

    Ask yourself: Is the caption formatted correctly according to course guidelines? If not, format the caption correctly.

6. Captions should **not refer to the picture as a picture** because those references are not useful.

    Ask yourself: Does the caption say something like, "This picture shows . . .." If so, revise the caption and avoid referring to the picture as a picture.

7. End captions with a well-formatted **citation** as needed.

    Ask yourself: Is the citation formatted according to course guidelines? If not, revise.

CHAPTER 2

Use topic sentence claims

With a strong emphasis on original thinking and argumentation, grading criteria for synthesis indicate a clear preference among instructors for topic sentences in academic writing that require supporting evidence. A preference for topic sentence claims among college instructors may be very different from expectations in high school if instructors only asked you to report general, factual information about readings.

> **General, factual topic sentence**
> *The wearable technology industry faces many problems.*
>
> **Targeted topic sentence claim**
> *A significant problem facing the wearable technology industry is a lack of usefulness in the devices.*

The first example also follows the common advice you might have received to move from general to specific in your paragraph development. In college writing, however, you want to start with a specific claim and move from specific to detailed in your paragraph developing, adding supporting evidence from credible sources so readers understand why you believe your claim is valid.

Support claims with valid source material

When you start a paragraph with a claim, you're making an assertion of belief, so to be persuasive, you also have to explain what your belief is based on. To give readers good reasons to agree with your beliefs, base your assertions on valid, relevant sources.

> Social media provides a new platform for police to track citizens' activity without their knowledge. **According to Daniel Trottier of the Department of Informatics and Media at Uppsala University**, social media remains a useful platform for policing due to social media's

CHAPTER 2

> importance in daily life and the vast amount of social media users. Trottier cites an example in Vancouver in 2011 where people protested after losing the Stanley Cup, a major tournament in Hockey. Many people expressed their opinions on social media by posting pictures and statuses of them protesting (Trottier 2012). Trottier stated that these pictures helped police track protesters and also helped police anticipate any moves. **Vancouver Police Department Sergeant Dave Wiedman stated** the police department had the names of suspects and locations (Trottier, 2012). While police had trouble sifting through numerous pieces of information, the fact that police use social media information proves that social media remains more instrumental in police investigations.

Draw original conclusions from analysis of multiple perspectives

Given the complexity of problems you explore in your courses, including many perspectives in your writing is an important practice.

> Animals in the world are constantly being threatened by the ever changing environment and weather. With these changing conditions comes extinction. It is estimated by the **UN Convention on Biological Diversity** that 150 different species go extinct each day (Pierce, 2015). With research in zoos it is possible to keep keystone species from going extinct. One main way that zoos study conservation is through **animal husbandry (Thompson, 1993, p. 159).** By studying methods of breeding, zoos can encourage the repopulation of certain species that are endangered. By researching conservation zoos can not only contribute to the conservation of species but also help educate the public.

Use signal phrases to introduce source material

Using signal phrases is a very effective way of signaling to readers that you're synthesizing what you've read. A signal phrase signals that you're integrating source material into your work.

CHAPTER 2

According to Dr. Margie Huerta, Executive Director of the National Hispanic Heritage Center....

Dr. Kelechi Onwuka, a researcher at Procter & Gamble, found that....

Quote, summarize, or paraphrase valid source information as required

Requirements for the use of source information indicate an instructor's preferences for how you should integrate others' ideas with your own. Because teammates have different experiences with research and synthesis, teams are much more productive when everyone uses source information correctly. Some instructors may want to see all source information paraphrased, others might prefer short quotations, interview transcripts, large block quotations, or other formats.

Include citations to indicate where your use of source material ends

In-text citations—those parenthetical or bracketed insertions in paragraphs that contain source information—have a practical purpose of indicating where to find the complete reference citation at the end of the work. A second practical purpose is to mark where source information ends, whether the information is in the form of a quotation, summary, or paraphrase.

Include evaluative conclusions that explain the significance and value of source material

Another way to meet objectives for synthesis is to end paragraphs with your own conclusions about why information in the paragraph is important. If you start the paragraph with a claim and include supporting evidence, you have done part of the work of synthesizing. To meet synthesis requirements for relating source information to a thesis or a topic sentence claim, add comments that explain how source information relates to your topic sentence or thesis.

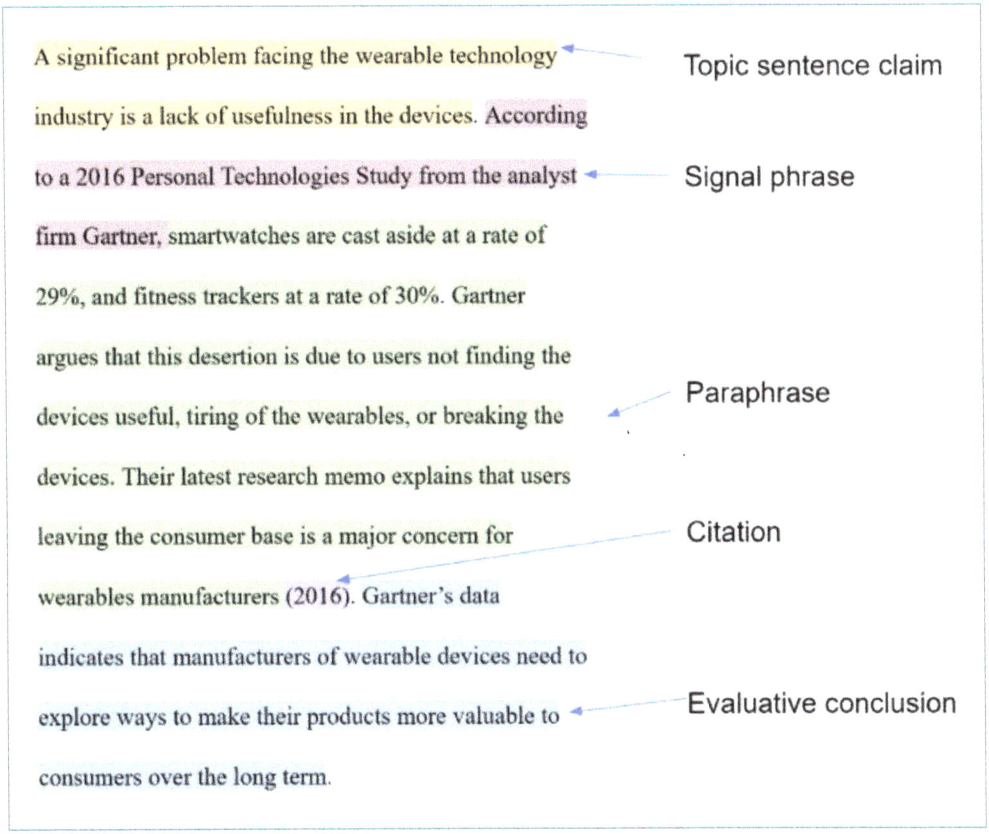

CHAPTER 2

A significant problem facing the wearable technology industry is a lack of usefulness in the devices. According to a 2016 Personal Technologies Study from the analyst firm Gartner, smartwatches are cast aside at a rate of 29%, and fitness trackers at a rate of 30%. Gartner argues that this desertion is due to users not finding the devices useful, tiring of the wearables, or breaking the devices. Their latest research memo explains that users leaving the consumer base is a major concern for wearables manufacturers (2016). Gartner's data indicates that manufacturers of wearable devices need to explore ways to make their products more valuable to consumers over the long term.

- Topic sentence claim
- Signal phrase
- Paraphrase
- Citation
- Evaluative conclusion

Figure 2.9. While paragraphs in academic writing can take many forms, one common structure consists of the five elements labeled above.

CHAPTER 2

> **Paragraph structure summary**
>
> When paragraphs include the following kinds of information, they go a long way toward meeting requirements for synthesis in research papers.
>
> 1. A topic sentence claim. That is, a topic sentence in the form of a debatable claim, which is a statement that some people might disagree with so requires support that shows what makes the claim valid. Debatable claims raise the question of Why? or How?
> 2. Signal phrases to introduce information from sources—specifically to emphasize the source's credibility.
> 3. Source information, paraphrased, that supports your topic sentence claim.
> 4. Citation(s) that help readers find sources in the reference section.
> 5. An evaluative conclusion that explains why paragraph content matters or how it relates to your main argument.

Review/editing skills

Two skills go hand-in-hand when preparing a final work for presentation or publication: skills for reviewing the work, and skills for revising it. The better you become at giving valuable feedback to others, the better you become at improving your own work.

Grading criteria from across the curriculum

Grading criteria for review/editing vary by instructor and discipline, as the following examples illustrate, so reviewing requirements for review/editing with teammates is time well spent.

> Is free of errors in grammar, punctuation and spelling that seriously interfere with comprehension (sociology).

CHAPTER 2

Shows evidence of proofreading and editing to catch mechanical errors. Uses consistent verb tense and voice (organizational leadership, policy, and development).

Provides effective critique to student colleagues on early drafts (disheries, wildlife, and conservation biology).

In its multiple drafts, evidences thoughtful and substantive revisions that address all of the feedback provided by the instructor and apply that feedback to further revisions of the entire text (anthropology).

Emphasizes active, rather than passive, sentence construction (journalism and mass communication).

Learning objectives for review/editing

We've derived seven learning objectives for review/editing that align with grading criteria from across the curriculum.

If you have learned to review/edit on a team, you should be able to

1. Use keywords strategically.
2. Maintain a tone of voice that is appropriate to your audiences.
3. Cite sources correctly.
4. Maintain a checklist of editing ideas.
5. Check for completion of specific tasks.
6. Give specific, supportive, valuable feedback.
7. Revise to improve clarity and focus.

Use keywords strategically

During the review and final editing phase of team writing, teammates must agree on some of the terminology to use to ensure clarity and avoid confusion. When composing in groups, teammates naturally express their ideas in ways that differ from each other. When researching, taking notes, and drafting content, it makes sense that one teammate might use phrasing such as information architecture while another

CHAPTER 2

might use content architecture. In a team-written paper, one teammate might use the phrase racial politics and another identity politics to refer to the same topic.

During researching, annotating, and drafting activities, many differences in phrasing emerge. Those differences provide an excellent opportunity for teammates to reflect together on the meanings of key phrases and which meanings best support the purpose and requirements of their projects. By the time a team presents a complete draft of a work for review, questions about phrasing should have been decided. Some decisions might be easy to make. Others might require careful consideration. In any event, keeping a list of ideas as a reference and a summary of your discussion is a good idea.

> 11/4: We're talking mostly about racial politics so we'll use *racial* instead of *identity, personal, gender,* or *religious* unless a specific need arises for further discussion.

> 11/6: teammates think of information mostly as written information. Since we're talking about management of photos, graphs, and illustrations along with written information, we'll use *content architecture* throughout the project.

Keywords that appear early—in the title and introduction, for example—should also appear later in the work. Repeating keywords in headings and subheadings is also a good practice because that strategic kind of repetition helps to ensure you're staying focused on central concepts.

Short, effective repetition keeps readers focused, too. Using keywords inconsistently, however, can result in confusion.

Maintain a tone that is appropriate to your audience and purpose

Much like word choice, the tone of voice you use is likely to vary by teammate—ranging from what some might perceive as very informal to very formal and everywhere between. Teammates' ideas of appropriateness are likely to vary widely, and given the diversity of cultures in many teams, more than one definition of appropriateness may be acceptable. It's less important to dictate to teammates what tone or attitude to take than it is to discuss a range of possible choices.

CHAPTER 2

Tone in published works is the result of several communication elements that when combined, project an attitude toward topics and audiences.

Common attitudes assigned in projects

- Neutral
- Objective
- Impersonal
- Angry
- Irreverent
- Insistent
- Urgent
- Funny
- Enthusiastic
- Respectful
- Sympathetic
- Anxious

Most professional and academic writing asks you to avoid colloquial language in order to achieve a level of seriousness that is appropriate to the topic. Instructors, assignments, and disciplines vary in their expectations, however, so the following examples might not be inappropriate in some cases:

> *The valuing of options contracts is all about determining the probabilities of future price events.*
>
> *The solution was super helpful because it saved the community $10,000.*
>
> *Since the 1980s, technology has been a huge influence on society.*
>
> *Wearable technologies affect us in our everyday lives in many ways, but for the sake of this project, we stuck to how they affect us in our professional lives.*

CHAPTER 2

Use citation formatting efficiently

In-text citations are typically comprised of three kinds of information: author last name(s), publication date, and page number when available. Avoid unnecessary repetition by including in the in-text citation only the information that's not already provided in the paragraph.

(Last name, year, page number)	(Year, page number)
In their analysis of 1,000 technical communication job postings, researchers concluded that collaboration and time management ranked as the highest-valued personal characteristics of candidates (**Brumberger & Lauer, 2015, p. 237**).	In their analysis of 1,000 technical communication job postings, Eva **Brumberger** and Claire **Lauer** concluded that collaboration and time management ranked as the highest-valued personal characteristics of candidates (**2015, p. 237**).
(Page number)	(Year) . . . (page number)
In their **2015** analysis of 1,000 technical communication job postings, **Brumberger** and **Lauer** concluded that collaboration and time management ranked as the highest-valued personal characteristics of candidates (**p. 237**).	In their analysis of 1,000 technical communication job postings, Eva **Brumberger** and Claire **Lauer** (**2015**) concluded that collaboration and time management ranked as the highest-valued personal characteristics of candidates (**p. 237**).

Figure 2.10. Complete in-text citations can take more than one form.

No matter what form the in-text citation takes, the reference citation is the same:

> Brumberger, E., & Lauer, C. (2015). The evolution of technical communication: An analysis of industry job postings. *Technical Communication, 62*(4), 224–243.

CHAPTER 2

Check for completion of specific tasks

Given the complexity of writing generally and collaborative writing specifically, keeping track of editing ideas is difficult without keeping a list of tasks to complete before turning in your work.

Because it's rare for any two teammates to have exactly the same academic or professional interests, experience, and writing abilities, keeping just one master list of items to check is likely to grow too large for any team to use efficiently. That's why maintaining an individual checklist of editing ideas specific to your interests can be valuable.

Suppose your instructor has pointed out that your use of pronouns (for example, this, it, these) makes your writing vague or imprecise. Adding a note, "Replace pronouns," to your editing checklist will remind you of one important way to improve clarity in your writing. Keeping a separate list of editing ideas for each of your classes will help you remember important details when you need them. We've included a sample editing checklist in the appendix.

If your instructor addresses a comment to the whole team ("Check personal pronouns—she, he, and they—to avoid making assumptions when discussing scholars' research") each teammate can decide whether to add a reminder to their checklist.

Give specific, supportive, valuable feedback

Your peer review comments are important demonstrations of achievement in any course. Your comments not only reflect your knowledge of important writing principles; they also provide teammates with valuable reminders that help increase the value of your collaboratively written materials.

Not all peer review comments are equally valuable, however. If comments are vague, for example, they neither reveal your knowledge nor provide useful direction to others. Therefore you want to make your comments specific enough to be useful.

CHAPTER 2

In general, the most effective peer review comments have one or more of the following qualities:

- They are specific to a project requirement.
- They suggest how to meet a project requirement.
- They provide a justification, stating how a specific change would add value to the project.

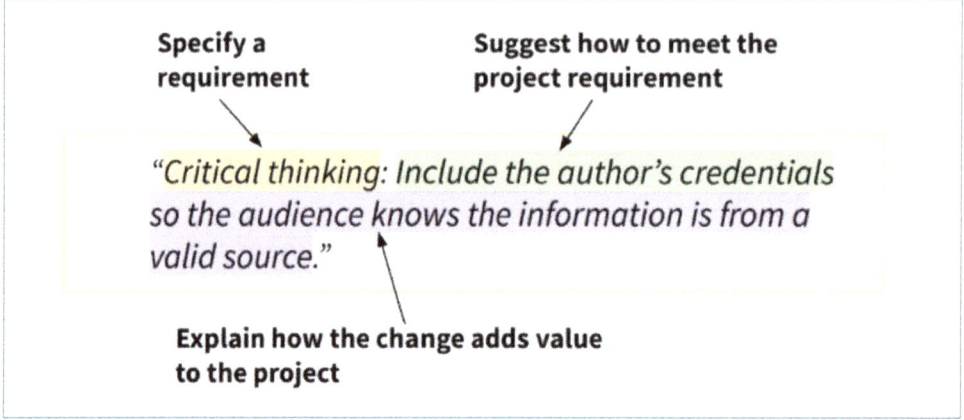

Figure 2.11. Detailed peer review comments help ensure your comments are useful and provide clear direction for revision.

Examples of valuable feedback

Reminds teammates of the need to define key terms—an important requirement.

> **Critical thinking:** *This is the first time anyone mentions "dual enrollment" in the paper, so include a short description of what it is so readers aren't confused.*

CHAPTER 2

Teammate accurately identifies achievement of a requirement. Emphasizing human impact is a research requirement.

> **Research:** *Nice job on highlighting how the problem affects people and why the problem needs to be addressed now.*

A relevant suggestion in a comment linked to specific text in the draft. The comment reminds the author of a specific project requirement.

> **Research:** *The research question should change to the form of: "What is the feasibility of doing X in order to achieve Y?"*

A relevant question in a comment linked to specific text in the draft. The question repeats an important project requirement.

> **Genre/structure:** *How does this observation relate to the research question or hypothesis?*

A relevant reminder to meet an important synthesis requirement.

> **Synthesis:** *Everyone should have some sort of in-text citation when they reference a source.*

A valid suggestion plus a valid rationale for following the advice.

> **Synthesis:** *Try to find a valid source that proves this point just to make this claim stronger.*

A valid suggestion that explains why the author should make the change.

> **Review/editing:** *We are focusing on children, not adolescents, so maybe change the wording.*

A good suggestion that includes a reason to make the change.

> **Review/editing:** *Better show the figure near the content. Make sure the audience understands what image you are talking about.*

CHAPTER 2

In the same way weightlifters rotate activities in order to stimulate different muscles, you develop the skills you need for writing to learn across the curriculum by rotating writing activities to stimulate different ways of problem solving. Skill groups, like muscle groups, build strength over time through a combination of repeating, resting, and taking on a variety of challenges.

Looking ahead

In the next chapter, you put the five skills into practice by completing specific tasks for writing projects and peer review.

CHAPTER 3

WRITING TASKS AND PEER REVIEW ROLES THAT MAKE YOUR TEAM PRODUCTIVE

GUIDING QUESTIONS

- How do defined tasks and roles make your writing team productive?
- What are high-priority writing tasks for teams?
- How do teams define teammate roles?
- How do teams assign teammate roles?
- How can teams use tasks and roles to gain feedback on their projects?

CHAPTER 3

Using tasks and roles to make your writing team productive

Productive collaboration requires well-defined roles so teammates are clear about who is responsible for making specific contributions to the project. Many textbooks suggest basic roles such as coordinator, researcher, editor, and designer or other roles that break writing projects up by function. Tasks and roles for collaborative writing projects in this book have some features in common with those basic roles but with one very important difference: instead of roles based on functions, roles in this book are based on learning objectives for your course.

The purpose of this chapter is to consider key writing tasks for projects. The tasks are the same whether you're writing material to contribute to a team project or to an individual writing project. The purpose of peer review is then to check on the team's achievements using the same criteria you used when performing the tasks.

> *Defining key terms*
> Collaboration is most productive when teammates agree on definitions of key terms. In this chapter, we use three key terms that are closely related but important to differentiate:
> **Learning objectives** are the knowledge and skills a project asks you to demonstrate.
> **Tasks** are what the project asks you to do in order to achieve learning objectives.
> **Roles** define groups of tasks the project asks you to perform during peer review.

Learning about tasks and roles prepares you for the workplace

In the workplace, hiring managers seek people who have a variety of expertise and experience so their organizations can create teams of people who approach problem solving from different perspectives. For example, a web-development team might consist of professionals that have varied roles––for example, a coder, a designer, a business analyst, and a usability specialist who create and test a website together. A business analyst's role is to think about sales goals and products to feature, a usability specialist thinks about users' interests and goals when visiting the site, the coder thinks about how to create functionality, and a designer's role is to think about page layout and visual design.

CHAPTER 3

By sharing ideas with each other from different professional perspectives, they learn about each other's ways of thinking about the website and quickly become productive based on what they learn together.

In the model we use in this chapter, you approach projects from different collaborative writing perspectives and become productive based on what you write and learn together.

Table 3.1. Writing and teamwork skills are transferable to other courses and to the workplace.

Main writing objectives	Main teamwork objectives
Critical thinking about problems and solutions.	Being consistently timely and clear in communications.
Writing focused research questions and hypotheses.	Consistently producing high-quality work to meet requirements and goals.
Organizing material according to professional practices.	Valuing inclusion and seeking positive team outcomes over just getting your own work done.
Drawing original conclusions from what you read.	Seeking to improve and helping others improve so team productivity increases.
Giving and receiving constructive feedback on projects.	Positively influencing the team, especially when facing challenges.

CHAPTER 3

Activity: Using collaborative writing skills to advance your goals upon graduating

1. Start by reviewing Table 3.1.
2. Describe a key professional goal you have, and then reflect on how the skills do and don't relate to that goal.

3. Discuss one of the most important writing and teamwork skills to you right now, and why.

4. Discuss one of the least important writing and teamwork skills to you right now, and why.

CHAPTER 3

Familiar writing tasks are surprisingly complex

One reason that productivity on writing assignments can falter is that it's so hard to see in advance all of the work you have to put into projects. Even the most simple-sounding assignments can turn out to require several tasks, so being aware of tasks helps you budget your time more realistically. If you're charged with writing a paragraph for a report, for example, that might seem like a fairly simple activity. When we outline tasks that you have to perform in order to write one paragraph, however, the assignment is clearly more demanding and time consuming than it may at first appear. Here's an example:

Goal: Write a paragraph for a team-written report

Tasks:

1. Find two valid, relevant sources on your topic. (A research task.)
2. Annotate the sources in order to identify content you can include in your paragraph. (A critical thinking task that involves multiple steps.)
3. Based on what you've read, write a claim that you can support with source material. (A synthesis task.)
4. Include information about each source's credibility to support readers' trust in the material. (A critical thinking task and, for many projects, a genre requirement.)
5. Quote, summarize, or paraphrase relevant source material. (A synthesis task.)
6. Include a well-formatted citation. (A research task.)
7. Write an evaluative conclusion about the significance of the examples. (A synthesis task.)
8. Proofread your work. (A review/editing task.)
9. Discuss how your paragraph meets project requirements with your teammates. (A collaboration task.)

CHAPTER 3

As the example above suggests, the complexity behind the most simple-sounding assignments can be significant. With that complexity in mind, we detail in this chapter the most common writing tasks for teammates.

Common writing tasks

Being aware of the many tasks that go into writing projects helps you accurately estimate how much time you need to work productively. As you review the list below, put a check mark next to the tasks that are familiar to you, and an X next to the unfamiliar ones.

Critical thinking tasks

- Address a targeted audience of readers.
- Make the purpose and audience of your work specific and clear.
- Define key terms.
- Include a counter-argument.
- Maintain credibility.

Research tasks

- Write a focused research question.
- State a hypothetical answer to your research question.
- Emphasize human impact and human interest in the topic.
- Describe cause and effect.
- Find sources that provide valuable information.

Genre/Structure tasks

- Include all relevant content.
- Orient readers with introductory information.

CHAPTER 3

- Include visual information.
- Format appropriately.
- Check for thoroughness and accuracy.

Synthesis tasks

- Make original claims and back them up with evidence from sources.
- Quote, summarize, or paraphrase as required.
- Use signal phrases as required.
- Include citations in APA format.
- Include evaluative conclusions.

Review & editing tasks

- Copyedit: correct errors and check for compliance with formatting requirements.
- Include and strategically repeat keywords.
- Use consistent, accurate terminology.
- Provide useful peer review.
- Proofread: a final check for minor errors.

> *When do teammates perform the tasks?*
> - All teammates perform the tasks when developing their own content.
> - Individual teammates perform role-specific tasks during peer review of team writing.

CHAPTER 3

Collaboration

When working collaboratively, a sixth set of tasks comes into play, which we detail in chapter four: Adaptation, cooperation, inclusion, participation, review, teamwork, and transparency.

Using objectives and tasks to guide content development and define peer review roles

> With well-defined learning objectives and tasks, you can now devise roles and responsibilities for teammates during peer review.

What roles are NOT

Teammate roles do not define the kinds of content each teammate should write for projects. The teammate in the research role is not solely responsible for doing the research for the team, for example. The teammate in the review/editing role is not solely responsible for proofreading, achieving technical accuracy, or performing other tasks commonly associated with review/editing.

What roles ARE

Roles correspond to objectives that all teammates should pursue while developing projects and drafting content. Teammate A is responsible for the quality of critical thinking, research, genre/structure, synthesis, review/editing in all of the work they contribute.

CHAPTER 3

> ## *What is peer review?*
>
> **Peer review** is an interdependent activity in which each teammate makes comments and suggestions related to one learning objective to help teammates complete tasks and achieve goals.
>
> **Interdependent** projects require contributions from all teammates in order to meet objectives. When no single person could realistically meet all objectives on their own, and when you count on others to contribute writing, insights, peer review, and other specific tasks to a project, you're working interdependently.
>
> **Increment review** is an informal presentation of a small part of the project (an increment) in which each teammate explains how a sentence, paragraph, image or other small part meets specific objectives of the project.

Instructions for peer review

Effective peer review requires attention to specific learning objectives and tasks. It's easy to get caught up in a lot of details when reviewing the project, so having a specific list of tasks helps you stay focused on high-priority objectives.

Using the tasks and roles to simplify peer review

Some students report that peer feedback they've received on their writing is very helpful, and some say peer feedback is not all that useful. Feedback tends to be most helpful when it raises relevant questions or includes reminders about important objectives of the project. The advantages of conducting thoughtful, focused peer review is that it benefits the person who's providing the feedback as much as the person who receives it.

CHAPTER 3

In the material that follows, we've included some questions you can ask during peer review that serve two primary purposes: 1) they help to make your peer review comments focused on key learning objectives, and 2) they remind you of key learning objectives to pursue in the content you contribute to the project.

1. Label your comments so teammates know which requirements you're discussing.
2. During review, start by identifying strengths. Where does the work meet requirements?
3. Avoid commenting on grammatical or spelling errors. Highlighting them is usually sufficient, and there's no need to mark up every instance of the same problem or even every type of different problem.
4. Make internal comparisons––that is, refer to content within the same document that represents comparatively high or low achievement. "This paragraph doesn't seem as detailed as many of your paragraphs––paragraph 4 is especially thorough and interesting, so you could add more detail here to make it as good as paragraph 4." "Your analysis on page 6 includes references to two similar studies, which made your conclusion persuasive. This later analysis doesn't reference other studies, so it seems less effective." "Would it work to use the same phrasing here as you used on page 2 so your wording is consistent?"

> *Project definitions*
>
> Because every course, project, and team is unique, keeping track of important definitions helps you stay productive while developing content and conducting peer review for team projects.
>
> **Requirements** are specific criteria for measuring the value of your writing. High achievement in each learning objective is the result of meeting requirements.
>
> **Value** refers to the benefits that readers realize from your attention to requirements. The value of including definitions of key terms in your writing, for example, is that readers benefit from having a shared understanding with you, the author.

CHAPTER 3

Critical thinking role for peer review

The teammate in the critical thinking role focuses on specific critical thinking requirements in their peer review of the entire draft. Use the spaces to revise or augment the criteria provided according to course requirements.

Critical thinking means attention to audience, purpose, definition, counter-argument, author and source credibility.

1. **Audience:** *Audience* refers to your intended readers—persons who need your work so they can make informed decisions.

During peer review:
- Highlight words that don't seem appropriate for the audience.
- Remind teammates of missing keywords.
- Suggest a change in tone when required.

CHAPTER 3

2. Purpose: The reason for writing to your audience.

During peer review:
- Look for a clear statement of purpose.
- Suggest where a purpose statement should be placed.
- Remind teammates of the purpose of the project.

3. Definition: 1) Content should address a well-defined topic; 2) define terms as needed so non-specialists can understand all words.

During peer review:
- Suggest where teammates should revise content so it more clearly defines project and paragraph topics.
- Suggest where teammates should define specific terms to avoid ambiguity.
- Check for definitions of technical terms to ensure teammates demonstrate understanding as required by the assignment.

CHAPTER 3

4. Counter-argument: Does the project spell out limitations of its main claim? Does it include perspectives from other sources about an alternative course of action to the one you're discussing? It should.

During peer review:
- Remind teammates of the need for a counter-argument, as required.
- Suggest where to place a counter-argument.
- Is the counter-argument thorough? If not, suggest additions.

5. Credibility: Trust based on the content you include and the manner in which you include it. You maintain credibility by serving readers' interests and citing relevant, trustworthy sources.

During peer review:
- Look for signal phrases for all source material, and remind teammates to add signal phrases as required.
- Point out content that may undermine credibility, such as weak sources and broad, unfounded claims.
- Suggest places where the addition of a citation would improve credibility.

CHAPTER 3

Research role for peer review

The teammate in the research role focuses on specific research requirements in their peer review of the entire draft. Use the spaces to revise or augment the criteria provided.

Research means attention to research questions, hypotheses, human impact, cause/effect, methods, results, and discussion.

1. Research question: What is the required format for a valid research question on this project?

During peer review:

- Review and comment on the format of the research question.
- Remind teammates of all required elements of the research question for this project.
- Suggest refinements for identifying or clarifying the research question.

CHAPTER 3

2. Hypothesis: State a hypothetical answer to your research question.

During peer review:
- Review and comment on the format of the hypothesis.
- Remind teammates of all required elements of the hypothesis for this project.
- Suggest refinements for identifying or clarifying the research question.

3. Human impact for the report refers to the measurable effects of the problem you're researching on the people who face it.

During peer review:
- Identify where the measurable effects appear.
- Remind teammates to add measurable effects when needed.
- Suggest additions that clarify types, frequency, and degree of human impact.

CHAPTER 3

4. Cause/effect refers to the impact of problems and solutions on specific groups of people. You should detail specific cause/effect examples to illustrate specific ways that a problem or a solution will affect those involved.

5. Sources should provide research value.

During peer review:

- Identify and comment on places where the author discusses the value of source material.
- Remind teammates to discuss the value of source material when needed.
- Suggest additions that clarify the value of source material.

CHAPTER 3

Genre/structure role for peer review

The teammate in the genre/structure role focuses on specific genre/structure requirements in their peer review of the entire draft.

Genre/structure means attention to required content and organization.

1. Content: The work should include all required content, organized appropriately.

During peer review:

- Look for all required content, and remind teammates of missing sections.
- Suggest where headings would add value by making the work scannable.
- Suggest reorganization of content to improve focus and clarity.

CHAPTER 3

2. Introduction: The work should properly orient readers to genre, content, and purpose.

During peer review:

- Look for required introductory information and remind teammates of missing information.
- Look for a statement of purpose and remind teammates to include missing information.
- Look for additional orienting information and remind teammates to include missing information.

3. Visual information should add value.

During peer review:

- Check for appropriate size and clarity of images.
- Check for captioning and citation requirements for images, tables, illustrations and other visual content.
- Look for information about the value of visuals, and remind teammates to include it when it's missing.

CHAPTER 3

4. Formatting: Check on requirements for length and type characteristics

During peer review:

- Remind teammates of length requirements.
- Identify errors in formatting (line spacing, type size, and use of paragraph styles), and recommend improvements.
- Check in-text and reference citation formatting and recommend improvements.

5. Value: Thoroughness, accuracy, appropriateness of content in all the sections.

During peer review:

- Point out relative thoroughness of different sections, and suggest additions where needed.
- Identify content that undermines the value of the work and raise questions about it.
- Remind teammates of content that would add value to the work.

CHAPTER 3

Synthesis role for peer review

The teammate in the synthesis role focuses on specific paragraph/idea development requirements in their peer review of the entire draft. Use the spaces to revise or augment the criteria provided.

Synthesis means attention to claims, signal phrases, paraphrasing, citations, evaluation and interpretation of course content, readings, and sources.

1. Claims: Review claims and look for sufficient support for claims from valid sources.

During peer review:

- Highlight topic sentences that sound more like facts than claims and remind teammates to start paragraphs with claims.
- Look for keywords in topic sentences and other claims, and recommend key words to repeat to maintain content focus.
- Remind teammates that claims should relate to your research question or hypothesis to some degree.

CHAPTER 3

2. Quotations, summaries, and paraphrases: Review for appropriate format according to project requirements.

During peer review:

- Check requirements for use of source material: can it be quoted, should it be summarized or paraphrased? Identify source material that's in the wrong format and remind teammates of the correct format.
- Check for quotation marks at beginning and end of quoted material as required.
- Help teammates avoid plagiarism by reminding them of project requirements.

3. Signal phrases: Signal the use of source material by naming the author, and at the first mention of the author, the signal phrase must include information about the author or the research team and what their credentials are.

During peer review:

- Check for signal phrases—remind teammates to use them as required.
- Point out where they're missing.
- Suggest ways of indicating author credibility.

CHAPTER 3

4. In-text citations: To indicate the ending point of source material, include a well-formatted citation.

During peer review:
- Check for consistent use of in-text citations, and remind teammates to use them.
- Point out where in-text citations are missing.
- Remind teammates of the correct format for in-text citations.

5. Evaluative conclusions: At the end of paragraphs, briefly summarize why information in the paragraph is important.

During peer review:
- Suggest the addition of evaluative conclusions where needed.
- Raise questions about the value of information in paragraphs.
- Point out effective evaluative conclusions.

CHAPTER 3

Review & editing role for peer review

The teammate in the review and editing role focuses on specific review and editing requirements in their peer review of the entire draft. Use the spaces to revise or augment the criteria provided.

Review/editing means being mindful of project requirements and adding notes that will help your teammates achieve goals of the project.

1. Style: Revise or raise questions about wording or phrasing.

During peer review:

- Highlight words whose meaning you're unsure about, and suggest teammates define or revise unclear words.
- Highlight phrases or sentences that don't seem clear and raise questions about them.
- Use suggestion mode (track changes) to give teammates alternative ways of phrasing.

CHAPTER 3

2. Word search: Ensure keywords are present and inaccurate words are not.

During peer review:

- Search for keywords from the assignment or your topic and remind teammates to use ones that are missing.
- Search for vague words such as thing, major, and this, and suggest revisions to improve clarity.
- Search for "etc." Unless it refers to specific ideas previously included in the work, replace "etc." with specific ideas.

3. Consistent, accurate wording: Choose words purposefully to maintain clarity and focus.

During peer review:

- If someone refers to "the problem of zebra mussels" at the beginning of the report and "the issue of invasive species" at the end, revise or make a note to say the phrasing is inconsistent.
- Check for repetition of keywords and suggest use of keywords when needed.
- Raise questions about the accuracy and consistency of wording in your comments.

CHAPTER 3

4. Supporting teammates who are multilingual learners: Having a conversation about all teammates' preferences for peer review helps to manage expectations. Do some teammates want you to revise their work? Would they prefer that you not revise their work?

During peer review: Depending on the preferences of students who have less experience in English than native speakers—

- Don't revise or delete the work of teammates who are multilingual learners.. Ask clarifying questions instead.
- If you find grammar or spelling errors, you can just highlight them to draw the teammate's attention. Label the comment "Review/editing."
- Making significant changes to others' work without permission is not respectful. In many cases, merely highlighting words or phrases to draw attention to them is sufficient. The teammate will take a look, think about what the issue might be, and revise. But again, no need to mark up wording or phrasing of multilingual writers unless it's requested.

CHAPTER 3

5. **"Choppiness":** With several teammates contributing to the report, some content might sound choppy, as if it were dropped onto the page without enough context for readers to understand its meaning or purpose. In the flurry of activity that goes with having several teammates adding to a project, you might write or paste in a passage intending to come back later to add transitions and avoid a change of topic that readers will find difficult to follow. If you forget to go back, or don't consider how what you've added might affect the logical progression of ideas, then the stream of ideas can get chopped up and readers can get lost.

During peer review: Depending on the preferences of students who have less experience in English than native speakers—

- If that happens, highlight the beginning of the content that sounds choppy and make a comment such as, "Review/editing: How do you see this information fitting with the previous content? Please add or revise a sentence so we can see the connection between what you've added and what came before (or after) it."
- Add or suggest headings that help orient readers to the topic of each section.
- Look for opportunities to reorganize content that seems out of place.

CHAPTER 3

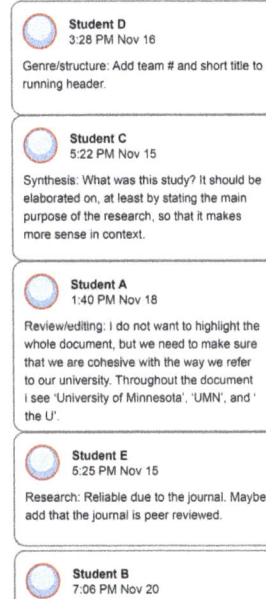

Figure 3.1. Labeling your peer review comments helps ensure your comments are targeted and useful.

CHAPTER 3

Increment review

Following the iterative design philosophy of design thinking, increment review offers teams a way to gather immediate, contextual feedback during—and not at the end of—the writing process. The purpose of increment review is to take stock of the team's progress and provide direction early and often. Increment reviews focus on small (hence increments) parts of the project.

Like peer review of an entire draft of a work, increment review asks teammates to complete role-specific tasks. Instead of commenting on the draft and addressing your comments to teammates, increment review is an informal presentation activity in which teammates take turns discussing ways in which a small part of their project meets specific objectives. During the review, teams have a chance to compare their project with others' and receive feedback from the instructor and classmates.

Increments might include a thesis, a paragraph, an image, an introduction, or any other small part of the project your team considers finished.

Reviewers then raise questions and provide feedback based on their understanding of project goals and objectives.

CHAPTER 3

Instructions for increment review

What to prepare: use slides or post-it notes or handouts, or share a document. For collaborative projects, all teammates should discuss the same increment.

What to discuss: each teammate takes one of the following roles and explains how the increment meets the most relevant objectives. Teammates may collaborate on creating explanations, but each teammate must present at least one explanation.

Use the spaces here to revise or augment the criteria provided.

If you have the **critical thinking** role, discuss how the increment meets critical thinking requirements for . . .

. . . *audience*

. . . *purpose*

. . . *definition*

. . . *counter-argument*

. . . *credibility*

CHAPTER 3

If you are in the **research** role, discuss how the increment meets research requirements for . . .

. . . the research question

. . . hypothesis

. . . human impact

. . . cause and effect

. . . sources

CHAPTER 3

If you are in the **genre/structure** role, discuss how the increment meets genre/structure requirements for . . .

. . . content

. . . introduction

. . . visual information

. . . formatting

. . . value

CHAPTER 3

If you are in the **synthesis** role, discuss how the increment meets synthesis requirements for . . .

. . . claims

. . . quotations, summaries, and paraphrases

. . . signal phrases

. . . in-text citations

. . . evaluative conclusions

CHAPTER 3

If you are in the **review/editing** role, discuss how the increment meets review/editing requirements for . . .

> . . . style

> . . . word search

> . . . consistent, accurate wording

> . . . supporting teammates who are multilingual learners

> . . . "choppiness"

CHAPTER 3

Examples of increment review explanations, by role

Critical thinking

"As the research question points out, the purpose of our report is to explore the feasibility of increasing boat inspections, so we will include studies of how effective boat inspections have been in other lakes in order to make our conclusions credible. Because we are writing for an audience of non-specialists, we will define terms used by the Minnesota Department of Natural Resources such as 'substrate' and 'veligers.'"

Research

"Our initial hypothesis, in answer to the research question, is that boat inspections are effective but that additional funding is needed so more boats can be inspected more often on Lake Minnetonka, and that the increased number of inspections will reduce the population of zebra mussels. To demonstrate cause and effect, we will research past studies to see whether increasing the number of inspections has in fact reduced populations in other lakes."

Genre/structure

"Our report will introduce the human impact of zebra mussels, describe our methods for gathering information from the MN DNR, The National Research Council, the Institute of Ecosystem Studies, and other sources. Methods will also describe the purpose of those studies so readers can tell why and how their studies were conducted. Our results will report factual information about the effect of increasing boat inspections. Our discussion will explain how the results of our research apply to the specific case of Lake Minnetonka and whether the same course of action is feasible."

CHAPTER 3

Synthesis

"Our research question enables us to make claims about the causes of zebra mussels and the effects they have on lakes, including the costs to Minnesota taxpayers, business owners, and the people who like to use the lake for recreational purposes. We'll incorporate our source materials and draw conclusions from our research so several paragraphs include evaluative conclusions about the feasibility of decreasing zebra mussels by increasing the number of boat inspections."

Review/editing

"The research question spells out specific ideas for making the proposal and report effective. For example, an effective proposal should explain that we plan to show how boat inspections actually make a difference to the population of zebra mussels. That's a strong claim about cause and effect. For the report to be effective, everyone needs to make contributions, and because the research question is appropriately complex for this assignment, it's likely that teammates will use differing terminology, so the person in the review/editing role will be able to add value to the report by looking for key terms and making sure that they are used accurately and consistently."

Follow-up questions

After an increment review, the instructor or classmates can ask follow-up questions to further the conversation.

Critical thinking follow-up questions

- What do you think is the most important argument your increment needs to make?
- What is the most convincing fact about the impact of the problem you have found so far?
- What is a key obstacle to solving the problem you're exploring and to what degree does your solution address that obstacle?
- What kinds of information have been most useful to you so far? Charts, descriptions, personal stories, survey data or other? What makes them useful?

CHAPTER 3

- What obstacles have you encountered as you prepared your increment for review from the perspective of critical thinking?

Research follow-up questions

- What is your research question and how do your research methods help you answer it?
- Which information have you found that shows how urgent the problem is for a specific group of people?
- What is your current hypothesis about the main cause of the problem you are exploring?
- What is your current hypothesis about a viable solution to the problem?
- What obstacles have you encountered as you prepared your increment for review from the perspective of research?

Genre/structure follow-up questions

- Which genre objective(s) does this increment address? That is, which part/section of the final doc(s) is this increment for? How does it meet objectives for that section?
- Which content objectives does this increment address? Which content objectives do you still have to meet at this point?
- How does this increment relate to other sections of the final project document(s)—is it introductory; is it a key claim that supports your main argument; is it supporting information for a key claim; is it your thesis?
- Based on organization objectives, is information from this increment likely to appear more than once in your final document? Why or why not?
- What obstacles have you encountered as you prepared your increment for review from the perspective of genre/structure?

CHAPTER 3

Synthesis follow-up questions

- How does your increment represent synthesis of ideas from your readings into ideas of your own?
- Where does the increment you've presented fit into the larger document? Is it introductory, for example; does it belong in methods, results, or discussion?
- Would you say your increment is primarily interpretive—discussing the significance of something—or evaluative—discussing the value of something?
- How are you as a team planning for high achievement in synthesis?
- What obstacles have you encountered as you prepared your increment for review from the perspective of synthesis?

Review/editing follow-up questions

- How does your increment meet objectives for review/editing for this project?
- What obstacles to achieving accuracy, consistency, and correctness do you anticipate?
- What obstacles to achieving accuracy, consistency, and correctness have you encountered so far?
- How are you as a team planning for high achievement in review/editing?
- What obstacles have you encountered as you prepared your increment for review from the perspective of review/editing?

CHAPTER 3

Peer review conversation

For some students, peer review is familiar. For others, it's not. Taking a little time to discuss the purpose of peer review and to learn about teammate preferences helps everyone work productively. Prior to conducting peer review, have a conversation with teammates about how your team will work together to improve the project.

Working alone

Reflect on how you feel about providing peer review comments.

- Are you comfortable responding to your teammates' writing? Are you unsure about the purpose of peer review?
- What questions do you have about the peer review process?
- What is your peer review role?
- How confident are you that you understand the learning objectives and tasks of your role? What questions or concerns about your role do you want to share with your teammates?
- Your team should come to an agreement about editing practices. What are your preferences?

Make thinking visible

Using the checklist in Figure 3.2, take turns sharing preferences, questions, or concerns with your small group.

Summarize your discussion in the team charter.

CHAPTER 3

If a teammate wants to...	They should...	
Correct spelling errors	Make changes ☐	Suggest only ☐
Delete something I've written	Make changes ☐	Suggest only ☐
Move something I've written	Make changes ☐	Suggest only ☐
Revise something I've written	Make changes ☐	Suggest only ☐
Add to something I've written	Make changes ☐	Suggest only ☐
Additional preferences	Make changes ☐	Suggest only ☐
Additional preferences	Make changes ☐	Suggest only ☐

Figure 3.2. Discussing teammate preferences for review and editing of each other's work helps manage expectations and avoid surprises.

CHAPTER 3

Summary

> You can use the same learning objectives to guide content development, peer review, and source annotations.

Using the same criteria for annotating sources as for drafting and peer review increases the amount of practice you gain in pursuing course objectives. In addition, the notes you take while reading will be useful when drafting content for your writing projects.

We outline the opportunities for focused practice with learning objectives in Table 3.2.

Table 3.2. Using the same criteria for teammate roles during content development, peer review, annotating, and instructor response increases student focus on course learning objectives.

For students			
When developing content for the project	**When peer reviewing teammate writing**	**When presenting an increment review**	**When annotating sources**
Ask how all content meets one or more objectives.	From the perspective of one role, ask how content meets project objectives.	Explain how the increment meets one set of learning objectives.	Take note of content and strategies to use, emulate, or reference.

CHAPTER 3

In review

- Defined tasks and roles make teams productive by helping teammates avoid unnecessary repetition of the same tasks by different teammates. They also help ensure that teams remember to pay attention to all the requirements.
- Basing team roles and tasks on course-specific learning objectives helps teams set priorities and stay focused on key activities.
- Teams have several opportunities for changing roles during projects so everyone has a chance to practice a variety of skills.

Looking ahead

In the next chapter you will learn how an interdependent writing environment for teams supports team productivity, and how to structure team meetings helps everyone meet key project objectives.

CHAPTER 4

COLLABORATION SKILLS FOR WORKING AND LEARNING IN TEAMS

GUIDING QUESTIONS

- How can teams adapt to change during projects?
- How does cooperation support collaborative writing?
- How can inclusion be woven into the decision-making process?
- How can teams measure participation?
- How does frequent review of team activities support collaboration?
- What does "pursuing shared goals" look like in practice?
- How do teams use transparency to support their goals?

CHAPTER 4

> We focus on the seven skills in this chapter because they all support one feeling teams rely on to be successful: **trust**.

Everyone on a writing team plays a role in making the experience a positive one. All students report a variety of fears about writing, whether they're writing individually or in teams, so making the classroom and team interactions safe for learning is a top priority. One student comment sums up a common feeling of vulnerability and a very positive outcome of working in teams:

> *I worried about the response I would get from my groupmates. To my surprise, I generally received positive feedback on my review comments with some constructive criticism from my teammates and instructor. It was overall a very enlightening experience for me and taught me not to be so afraid of conquering new tasks.*

As an individual, you can make positive contributions to your team while developing these seven valuable skills:

- **Adaptation:** Welcoming change based on what you learn about course content, teammates, and yourself.
- **Cooperation:** Responding to teammates' requests for information and questions about projects.
- **Inclusion:** Inviting, welcoming, and considering perspectives of all teammates in activities and decision making.
- **Participation:** Actively attending meetings, updating memos, completing work, sharing ideas, making suggestions
- **Review:** Staying current with retrospectives, project visions, peer review and revision, and updates to the team charter.
- **Teamwork:** Pursuing shared goals with a positive attitude.
- **Transparency:** Making your thinking visible; sharing concerns.

CHAPTER 4

Adaptation: Welcoming change based on what you learn about course content, teammates, and yourself

Adaptation is an attitude and set of skills that enables you to change during projects. What you learn while reading, writing, and talking with teammates may result in significant changes to your attitudes, knowledge, values, or ways of thinking, and adapting to those changes isn't always automatic.

Adaptation skills include the ability to

- Acknowledge from the start and accept that group members might not always agree.
- Break old habits that no longer work.
- Continuously improve.
- Identify possible reasons for plans not going as expected and propose possible adaptations.
- Revise substantially based on what you learn from instructor and peer review.
- Weigh ideas against project requirements instead of personal preference.
- Work productively in the face of uncertainty.

Cooperation: Responding to teammates' requests for information and questions about projects

Cooperation is a relational skill that lets teammates know they can trust you and that you respect them.

Cooperation skills include the ability to

- Keep update memos current to avoid surprises.
- Maintain a positive attitude; avoid blaming; focus on solutions instead of problems.
- Maintain a professional tone (avoiding impatience, anger, frustration).
- Notify teammates and instructor as soon as possible when you can't be in class or attend meetings or meet commitments on time.
- Share resources that assist others.

CHAPTER 4

- Take suggestions without defensiveness.
- Respond to communications in an agreed-upon time frame with agreed-upon tools.

Inclusion: Inviting, welcoming, and considering perspectives of all teammates in activities and decision making

Inclusion results from paying attention to all teammates, their preferences, and ideas.

Inclusion skills include the ability to

- Act if you feel that someone's viewpoint is not being respected or heard.
- Include diverse voices instead of pursuing a "unified" voice.
- Invite, welcome, and weigh perspectives of all teammates before making decisions.
- Overcome personal biases.
- Practice inclusivity before efficiency.
- Share responsibility for inclusivity among all teammates.
- Value inclusivity over consensus.

Participation: Actively attending meetings, updating memos, completing work, sharing ideas, making suggestions

Showing up and being prepared tells teammates you're committed to the project.

Participation skills include the ability to

- Be prepared for class and team meetings.
- Challenge ideas respectfully. Share ideas without forcing them or dominating discussions.
- Complete a fair share of the work.
- Focus on requirements most of the time when making suggestions.
- Ask for help understanding requirements and how to meet them.
- Listen attentively; ask follow up question.
- Make contributions on time, complete.

CHAPTER 4

Review: Staying current with team documentation, peer review and revision, and updates to the team charter

Because project details can change quickly and frequently, continuous review helps you stay on track and reassures teammates that you have the latest information.

Review skills include the ability to

- Complete peer review on time.
- Make thorough, useful peer review comments and suggestions.
- Read assigned materials including project visions by due date so you know basic requirements.
- Revise, suggest, or comment according to team agreements for peer review.
- Reflect on what's working and what's not working, and make changes right away to improve inclusivity or productivity.
- Stay up to date on changes and additions to the team charter.
- Use checklists before submitting project work.

Teamwork: Attention to achieving shared goals

A key difference between individual writing and team writing is in the commitments you make. Teammates build trust by working toward shared goals.

Teamwork skills include the ability to

- Anticipate obstacles my team might encounter before we encounter them.
- Commit to meeting requirements (shared goals).
- Expect all teammates to contribute to all sections of a work.
- Make suggestions that serve shared goals (not exclusively your own goals).
- Provide a rationale to teammates for solutions you choose.
- Seek input from teammates when seeking a solution to a problem.
- Share leadership, provide leadership.

CHAPTER 4

Transparency: Making your thinking visible; sharing concerns

A primary goal of transparency is to help everyone on the team 1) make informed decisions and 2) avoid wasted effort that occurs because of false assumptions about teammates or project requirements.

Transparency skills include the ability to

- Add to shared documents by the due date.
- Ask questions when you're not sure about a requirement, task, or role.
- Contribute as soon as possible if you miss a meeting or class session.
- Express support for ideas you agree with.
- Notify teammates in advance when you can't meet deadlines.
- Raise concerns during discussions, retrospectives, and peer review.
- Tell your instructor or teammates when you need support.

Next-level inclusivity

A primary reason that instructors give for assigning group work is that students who work in teams are exposed to the diverse perspectives of their teammates. We subscribe to the same idea but add that inclusivity is a skill rather than an automatic outcome of group work.

If you've ever been reluctant to speak up in a group situation, you know what we mean. Students report a variety of reasons for their reluctance: fear of sounding stupid, fear of making a mistake, lack of experience, wanting more time to think before speaking, getting the feeling that their opinions aren't welcome.

Other students report not being sure how to invite others to contribute or participate: fear of being pushy, fear of sounding presumptuous, lack of experience, wanting to give others more time to think but not wanting to be seen as holding up the group; getting the feeling that someone else wants to be the leader of the group.

Given the challenges of achieving a truly inclusive environment for learning, teams benefit from frequent attention to norms aimed specifically at achieving inclusivity.

Norms for highly inclusive writing teams

- Act if you feel that someone's viewpoint is not being respected or heard.
- Include diverse voices instead of pursuing a "unified" voice.
- Invite, welcome, and weigh perspectives of all teammates before making decisions.
- Overcome personal biases.
- Practice inclusivity before efficiency.
- Share responsibility for inclusivity among all teammates.
- Value inclusivity over consensus.

Act if you feel that someone's viewpoint is not being respected or heard

Reaching goals for inclusivity requires that teammates pay attention to who speaks in your group and who doesn't, and everyone needs to make an effort to include others in conversations. In some cases, everyone might speak but not really be heard. When that happens, you can act by redirecting the conversation:

> "Before you make a second comment, let's hear from others who haven't weighed in yet."

> "I don't think you had a chance to finish your thought. Tell us more about what you were saying."

Redirecting attention to group norms or broader guidelines is also effective.

> "Let's stop a second and talk about norms for group discussions."

> "The syllabus has some guidelines for group discussions we need to review."

Include diverse voices instead of pursuing a "unified" voice

Another bias being debated in higher education is the favoring of one type of English language usage over others, with a preference for language practiced predominantly by white academics and professionals. Writing teams may or may not be charged with debating important ethical questions about language use and what standards to use. Many students go to college to learn a "right way to communicate," while others feel oppressed by being held to standards that are unfamiliar or seem arbitrary or exclusive.

Whatever the instructor's approach to language, and their expectations for unity, teams benefit from acknowledging that teammates bring a variety of experience with language to group work. Native speakers of English bring regional and ethnic language variations to the group as do multilingual teammates. So having a conversation about how and when to edit each other's work is a good idea. Some people appreciate suggestions for changing words, tense, and sentence structure, for example. Some prefer that teammates use a track changes or suggesting function; others are okay with teammates making changes directly to their writing.

Our suggestion is for teams to agree never to delete or move a teammate's contribution to a work before discussing it first. For one teammate to unilaterally remove someone else's work strikes us as being disrespectful and uncollaborative.

Invite, welcome, & weigh perspectives of all teammates before making decisions

Inclusive leadership emphasizes the invitation of multiple perspectives and suspension of judgment until the team considers several alternative directions.

Overcome personal biases

Working in teams often means collaborating with individuals you don't know very well. You don't know whether you have likes or dislikes in common, life experiences that are similar, familiar beliefs, or common interests. It's human nature to fill in blanks about others based on assumptions we form about people over time about abilities, attitudes, interests, and beliefs based on what we perceive to be others' identities.

There's an old riddle about a man and his son who are involved in a car accident. The father dies at the scene. The boy is injured and requires surgery, and when he's wheeled into the operating room, the surgeon looks down and says, "I can't operate on this boy—he is my son." How can that be, the riddle asks, and the answer is that the surgeon is the boy's mother. The riddle relies on a bias that says a person who is a surgeon must be a male.

Common biases in collaborative writing teams include the idea that people who are quiet don't have any ideas, that people who write more slowly are less accomplished than people who write quickly. Some people hold biases based on others' work preferences. For example, some people like to get their work done as soon as possible after it's assigned. Others are more deadline driven. A common bias we hear from people who like to do their work right away is that people who are deadline-driven dislike working with slackers who wait until the last minute. From those who prefer to finish their work near the deadline, we hear the claim that people who bug them about getting their work done early are pushy.

Personal bias extends to assumptions about people based on their race, ethnicity, gender, ability, sexual orientation, or religion. In the absence of other information, people may make assumptions about others' based on stereotypes—reductive beliefs held consciously or unconsciously about others' motives or abilities. Everyone can think of stereotypes without much effort. And because they're so common, they can feel you believe they're true or not, whether you judge people by them or not, whether you consider them to be positive or negative, and whether you have any idea where you learned them. Consider whether you're familiar with stereotypes about people who are

Black	Gay	Men	Republican	White
Chinese	Homeless	Mexican	Teenage	Women
Deaf	Jewish	Muslim	Transexual	Etc.
Democrat	Lesbian	Native American	Vegan	

Given that assumptions about others are very easy to make, biases come up in collaborative writing teams all the time, with effects that can affect individual abilities to fully develop important collaboration skills.

Overcoming personal biases is lifelong work—it's not something people can achieve in one project or one semester. But teammates can help each other maintain an environment for collaborative writing and learning by acknowledging that biases exist, by identifying them when they emerge, and by working toward deeper understanding of teammates.

Teammates who overcome personal biases

- Make an effort to be aware of their own biases.
- Risk being uncomfortable in order to address inequality.
- Think about the context in which they make comments about others.
- Say something if they feel that someone's viewpoint is not being respected or heard.
- Look for commonalities with teammates whose identities differ from their own.
- Be aware of whose perspectives are and are not being represented.

Share responsibility for inclusivity among all teammates

Making inclusivity a priority means sharing in the efforts to ensure all teammates are invited, welcomed, and respected. Teams committed to inclusivity make accommodations of space, time, and modes of communication to ensure all teammates are able to share ideas without being rushed.

Practice inclusivity before efficiency

When working in teams, rushing through conversations can be tempting. People run out of ideas or they want to get on to the next item on the agenda. "Let's move on" is the mantra.

Problems can arise when teams rush, however. Teammates who want time to process information before they weigh, teammates who want more time to learn, multi-lingual teammates who want more time to reflect don't get the time they need. As a result, those teammates may feel silenced or excluded. And when teams rush, unexplored "solutions" can take teams down paths that go in the wrong direction.

Sometimes moving quickly works, such as when discussing routine issues the team has addressed many times before. But when writing projects are just getting started, when course vocabulary is new, teammates are not yet acquainted with each other, and everyone is still learning project requirements, longer discussions are essential.

Value inclusivity over consensus

When compared with typical group agreements that value consensus, agreements that value inclusivity take a significantly different approach to decision making.

Practices in both columns have advantages and disadvantages. Pursuing consensus, for example, can lead to all teammates reaching the same understanding of a problem or a solution. Similarly, acting on majority preferences can be expedient while satisfying most teammates. Fixing practices and policies in advance can save time, and avoiding discussions of race and power prevents teammates from having difficult conversations or having ideas challenged.

Disadvantages of pursuing consensus include discouraging alternative solutions, and majority rule by definition identifies and may marginalize a minority of teammates. Fixed practices can short-circuit team ownership, and avoiding discussions about identity and power ignores important dimensions of team dynamics that can affect productivity and the value of the learning experience.

Typical group agreements	Inclusive group agreements
Pursues consensus (agreement)	Explores differences and disagreements as opportunities for learning
Majority rules in decision making	Decisions comprised of multiple perspectives & directions subject to review
Practices/policies are fixed in advanced	Practices/policies evolve
Power/race-neutral	Power and racial dynamics (inequity) is recognized (CEI, 2021).

Figure 4.1. Inclusive team agreements take into considerations differences, inequity, and power dynamics.

Weigh all ideas against project requirements

Being inclusive does not mean treating all ideas as equally valid, valuable, or useful. Inclusivity is an attitude of respect toward all teammates and a preference for ideas that meet project requirements.

CHAPTER 4

Next-level collaboration

One of the ways teams get better at collaboration is by periodically assessing each other's performance. To take your team to the next level of collaboration, have teammates complete a survey for everyone on the team.

Adaptation skills

Adaptation skills include the ability to:	Always	Often	Sometimes	Rarely
Continuously improve.	◎	◎	◎	◎
Revise substantially based on what you learn from instructor and peer review.	◎	◎	◎	◎
Break old habits that no longer work.	◎	◎	◎	◎
Identify possible reasons for plans not going as expected, and propose possible adaptations.	◎	◎	◎	◎
Acknowledge from the start and accept that group members might not always agree.	◎	◎	◎	◎
Work productively in the face of uncertainty.	◎	◎	◎	◎
Weigh ideas against project requirements instead of personal preference.	◎	◎	◎	◎

CHAPTER 4

Cooperation skills

Cooperation skills include the ability to:	Always	Often	Sometimes	Rarely
Maintain a professional tone (avoiding impatience, anger, frustration).	◎	◎	◎	◎
Take suggestions without defensiveness.	◎	◎	◎	◎
Share resources that assist others.	◎	◎	◎	◎
Respond to communications in an agreed-upon time frame with agreed-upon tools.	◎	◎	◎	◎
Keep update memos current to avoid surprises.	◎	◎	◎	◎
Maintain a positive attitude; avoid blaming; focus on solutions instead of problems.	◎	◎	◎	◎
Notify teammates and instructor as soon as possible when you can't be in class or attend meetings or meet commitments on time.	◎	◎	◎	◎

Inclusion skills

Inclusion skills include the ability to:	Always	Often	Sometimes	Rarely
Share responsibility for inclusivity among all teammates.	◎	◎	◎	◎
Invite, welcome, and weigh perspectives of all teammates before making decisions.	◎	◎	◎	◎
Act if you feel that someone's viewpoint is not being respected or heard.	◎	◎	◎	◎
Overcome personal biases.	◎	◎	◎	◎
Value diverse voices over a "unified" voice.	◎	◎	◎	◎
Practice inclusivity before efficiency.	◎	◎	◎	◎
Value inclusivity over consensus.	◎	◎	◎	◎

CHAPTER 4

Participation skills

Participation skills include the ability to:	Always	Often	Sometimes	Rarely
Be prepared for class and team meetings.	◎	◎	◎	◎
Listen attentively; ask follow-up questions.	◎	◎	◎	◎
Focus on requirements most of the time when making suggestions. Ask for help understanding reqs and how to meet them.	◎	◎	◎	◎
Make sure memo contributions are always on time, complete.	◎	◎	◎	◎
Challenge ideas respectfully. Share ideas without forcing them or dominating discussions.	◎	◎	◎	◎
Complete a fair share of the work.	◎	◎	◎	◎
Always present.	◎	◎	◎	◎

Review skills

Review skills include the ability to:	Always	Often	Sometimes	Rarely
Read assigned materials including project visions by due date so you know basic requirements.	◎	◎	◎	◎
Complete peer review on time.	◎	◎	◎	◎
Make thorough, useful peer review comments and suggestions.	◎	◎	◎	◎
Reflect on what's working and what's not working, and make changes right away to improve inclusivity or productivity.	◎	◎	◎	◎
Stay up to date on changes and additions to the team charter.	◎	◎	◎	◎
Use checklists before submitting project work.	◎	◎	◎	◎
Revise, suggest, or comment according to team agreements for peer review.	◎	◎	◎	◎

CHAPTER 4

Teamwork skills

Teamwork skills include the ability to:	Always	Often	Sometimes	Rarely
Commit to meeting requirements (shared goals).	◎	◎	◎	◎
Seek input from teammates when seeking a solution to a problem.	◎	◎	◎	◎
Provide a rationale to teammates for solutions I choose.	◎	◎	◎	◎
Anticipate obstacles my team might encounter before we encounter them.	◎	◎	◎	◎
Expect all teammates to contribute to all sections of a work.	◎	◎	◎	◎
Make suggestions that serve shared goals (not exclusively your own goals).	◎	◎	◎	◎
Share leadership, provide leadership.	◎	◎	◎	◎

Transparency skills

Transparency skills include the ability to:	Always	Often	Sometimes	Rarely
Add to shared documents by the due date.	◎	◎	◎	◎
Notify teammates in advance when you can't meet the deadline.	◎	◎	◎	◎
Raise concerns during discussions, retrospectives, peer review.	◎	◎	◎	◎
Contribute as soon as possible if you miss a meeting or class session.	◎	◎	◎	◎
Tell the instructor or teammates when needing support.	◎	◎	◎	◎
Ask questions when not sure about a requirement, task, or role.	◎	◎	◎	◎
Express support for ideas they agree with.	◎	◎	◎	◎

CHAPTER 4

Looking ahead

The next chapter introduces you to a human-centered approach to collaboration that includes five structured activities that support writing in teams.

CHAPTER 5

A PRODUCTIVE PROCESS FOR WRITING IN TEAMS

GUIDING QUESTIONS

- What are key activities in a productive collaborative writing process?
- How do teams know whether they're being productive?
- How can teams keep track of their work?
- How can teams improve productivity during projects?

CHAPTER 5

Writing, process, and collaboration

The collaborative writing process we detail in this chapter is a human-centered approach to writing in teams. We think about being human-centered in two ways, with one focused on the audience for the content you're creating and the other focused on the writers on the team. Paying attention to both the writing on the page and the writers on the team is important because the challenges of collaborative writing come not only from what you have to learn about the topic you're writing about and how to write about it; they also come from the communication, cooperation, and teamwork you have to achieve as a teammate.

A key advantage to writing in teams is that you can multiply the number of ideas to work with in the same amount of time it takes one person to come up with ideas by themselves. Nevertheless, ideas by themselves remain just ideas unless you explore and compare and develop them in a structured process for achieving a goal.

The collaborative writing process in this book includes six types of structured activities for writing in teams:

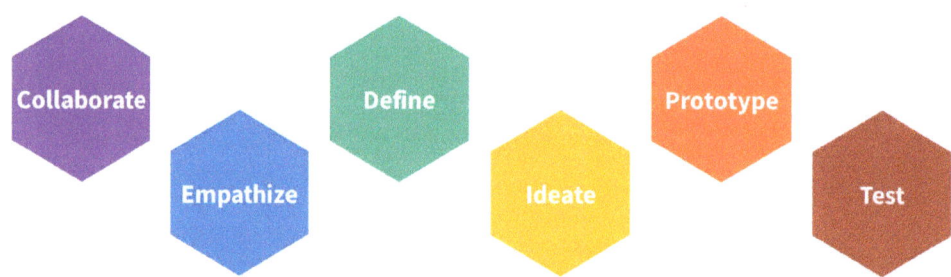

Figure 5.1. A modified design thinking process is well-suited to collaborative writing because it's an iterative, inclusive process. We've added "Collaborate" to make it an explicit feature of the process and to identify specific activities that support productive teamwork.

CHAPTER 5

Collaborating

As we discuss in Chapter 4, activites that support strong collaboration include adaptation, cooperation, inclusivity, participation, reviewing, pursuing shared goals (teamwork), and making thinking visible (transparency).

Empathizing

The original purpose of the empathizing phase of design thinking was to ask product designers to learn about their customers' needs and interests as an initial phase of new-product development. By understanding and sharing the feelings of customers, designers are able to improve the value and usability of the products they create.

In collaborative writing, empathizing with your audience is similarly valuable in helping you create interesting, useful, relevant information for others.

Given the complexities of collaborative writing, empathizing with teammates is a similarly powerful influence on project development. Learning how teammates feel about writing in a team, how they feel about the topic, how invested they are in the project all matter. For writing teams to be productive, they should pay attention to the writers on the team and the content on the page in order to avoid making false assumptions about each other that can undermine productive collaboration.

Defining

The defining phase of design thinking asks teammates to spend time thinking about problems in some detail instead of rushing to work on a solution. A variety of negative perceptions about collaborative writing can be linked to teams favoring expediency—taking the first idea that someone offers and running with it without any deliberation—over reflection and problem definition. A take-charge kind of teammate might float an idea, an outspoken teammate tosses out some others—and

CHAPTER 5

the rest of the team follows along for a variety of unexplored reasons. Therefore, defining problems and goals based on ideas from all teammates, and subjecting all ideas to discussion and assessment by comparing them to project objectives, is a valuable stage in the collaborative writing process.

Ideating

Call it brainstorming, idea generating, thinking outside the box, but whatever you call it, ideating is a time for reserving judgements and suspending your own personal preferences. In an ideating mindset, you're trying to come up with lots of ideas—not necessarily the most logical or practical or efficient ones.

Prototyping (making ideas visible)

A prototype is a rough model. It can be a sketch, a few words written by hand, some sentences, a wire frame for a web site, or other rough model of something you want to create. In some ways, a draft of a paper is a prototype because early in the writing process you're sketching out ideas, outlining or otherwise subjecting initial ideas for review and feedback from others. But long before you produce a polished draft, prototyping is a quick and easy way to put ideas into concrete form.

CHAPTER 5

Quick outlines	Basic drawings	Sticky notes

Title
• *Topic*
   ○ *Subtopic*
   ○ *Subtopic*
• *Topic*
• *Topic*
   ○ *Subtopic*
   ○ *Subtopic*		

Figure 5.2. Prototypes are quick and basic. They bring ideas to life in visual form so you can share them them others easily and gather ideas for further development.

Prototyping is a time for brainstorming possible solutions to the problem you've defined, discussing possible directions proposed by all teammates, agreeing on one that could work, and quickly drafting, sketching, or building a model that represents your team's direction for a possible solution. Individual expressions may be verbal or visual but all teammates should contribute if teams are to maximize the benefits of collaboration. Once the team has taken enough time to review all teammates' suggestions, choose one—or a composite or even new ideas that emerge during review—and develop it for review.

Testing

Testing is conducting various activities for assessing your written work and your productivity.

> **Team review:** explaining how content examples meet project requirements.
>
> **Team update meetings:** short meetings about what you've completed, what you plan to complete by the next meeting, what obstacles you encounter, and how you plan to overcome the obstacles.

CHAPTER 5

Team retrospectives: discussing what's working for the team, what's not working, and how to make changes right away to improve productivity.

Collaborative writing meetings

Team meetings and productivity go hand in hand. Whether meetings take place in class or outside of class, meetings give teammates a chance to check in with each other during the writing process to reflect on what you're doing and why.

Each type of meeting in the collaborative writing process has a unique purpose. For example, team update meetings are for coordinating everyone's efforts; team review meetings are for discussing how the work you're doing together meets specific project requirements; and team retrospective meetings are for teams to discuss their productivity and how to improve it.

Table 5.1. Brief, strategic meetings support productivity by promoting review, transparency, and adaptability.

Meeting	Agenda	Update memos
Team Update Length: 15 minutes When: Daily or as often as needed.	Share important updates with teammates. - Time spent, tasks completion percentage - What's finished? - What will you complete by the next meeting? - What obstacles have you encountered? - What obstacles do you anticipate encountering? - How will you work at overcoming obstacles?	Team update memo
Team Review Length: 15 minutes When: During prototyping.	**What to prepare:** An increment or excerpt for review: it may be words, phrases, sentences, titles, images, drawings, a definition, research question, thesis, subtitle, outline, single paragraph, or any other content representative of your progress. **What to discuss:** each teammate takes turns explaining the increment(s) from the point of view of a specific role/requirement. Teammates listen and respond with follow-up questions.	Team review memo including a summary of what you plan to do next based on the feedback you've received.
Team Retrospective Length: 15 minutes When: After team review and as needed.	What has been working well? What hasn't been working well? What will you do differently right away?	Team retrospective memo Teammate continuous improvement update

A conversation framework for meetings

The purpose of the conversation framework is to ensure a strategic process for team discussions during meetings (Bruffee, 1993, pp. 28-51). The opposite of what we're proposing here is a "discussion" in which the team agrees to take the first idea someone shares without exploring at length where that idea might lead the team.

Productive collaborative writing meetings that care about the content on the page and the writers on the team have four qualities:

1. They give all teammates time to work alone
2. They use ways of making thinking visible
3. They seek inclusion instead of consensus
4. They base decisions on project requirements

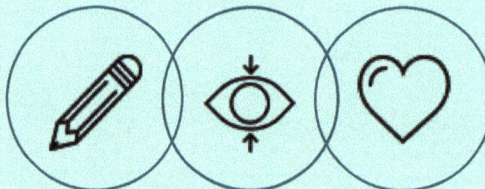

Figure 5.3. Having strategic conversations means suspending closure in favor of giving all teammates a chance to contribute prior to decision-making.

■ Working alone

People need different amounts of time to think and write, so building in time to work alone is a good way to start a conversation. While some teammates will have ideas to share right away, others will need time to gather their thoughts. If you're working in English and English is not the first language of some teammates, making time for the complex process of thinking plus translating gives everyone some time for reflecting.

■ Make thinking visible

Working on a shared document or using sticky notes or a whiteboard are all effective ways to make ideas visible.

■ Empathize with teammates and your audience

Teammates will have a variety of thoughts and feelings about the activity and topic and about sharing ideas with the group. Some people will feel uncomfortable and that feeling can come from lack of experience, fear of doing something incorrectly, not being used to participating in a group or many other reasons.

Teammates who are used to working in teams or have experience and confidence in their ideas might still experience some feelings of stress, impatience, or anxiety.

Keeping the possible range of feelings in mind and checking in with teammates is therefore an important part of collaboration.

CHAPTER 5

1. Team update meetings

Lasting only 15 minutes at most, update meetings are informal discussions about three questions:

1. What have you completed since the last meeting?
2. What do you plan to complete by the next meeting?
3. What obstacles to productivity are you encountering?

A few ground rules help ensure that update meetings are productive:

- All teammates take a turn to answer the questions.
- No phones or other devices in use; meeting times are not bathroom or snack breaks.
- All teammates are encouraged to be present.
- Teammates collaboratively write a team update memo after everyone has spoken.
- Team update memos about tasks completed or to be completed should be concrete and quantifiable: not "I wrote some stuff, but "I wrote 200 words on the topic of _____; I read eight pages of _____; I spent two hours researching the question of _____.
- A teammate is assigned or volunteers to notify absent teammates of the update memo activity requirements.

CHAPTER 5

Why 15-minute meetings?

To make team meetings productive, keep them focused. You can accomplish a lot in 15 minutes when you have a specific purpose, and each of the team meetings in the collaborative writing process is purpose driven. Meeting for longer periods of time can be difficult when coordinating teammate schedules, but having frequent but brief meetings gives everyone a chance to check in, get caught up, and prepare for next steps.

2. Team review meetings

Team review is an informal presentation of an increment of work that teams have developed. Increments that teams select for review should be brief. An increment is any kind of content that teams have created to meet project requirements: words, titles, images, sentences, headings, or paragraphs.

Each teammate should discuss how the increment addresses specific requirements of the project. For example, an instructor using the five basic requirement/role categories of critical thinking, research, genre/structure, synthesis, and review/editing, would ask students to discuss how an increment of their team's work meets requirements for each role. During the review, teams receive feedback and have a chance to compare their project with other teams' work. The length of team review meetings may vary depending on where you are in the project, but at minimum, teams should address questions about ways the increment meets or attempts to meet project requirements.

CHAPTER 5

Critical thinking role	Explain how the increment addresses critical thinking requirements for the project.
Research role	Explain how the increment addresses requirements for research.
Genre/structure role	Explain how the increment addresses requirements for genre, content, organization—specifically with respect to the assigned genre.
Synthesis role	Explain how the increment addresses requirements for synthesis.
Review/structure role	Explain how the increment addresses requirements for spelling, grammar, and style.
Collaboration role	Explain how the increment addresses requirements for adaptation, cooperation, inclusivity, review, teamwork, and transparency.

Figure 5.4. The goal of team reviews is to present small increments of writing and discuss how they meet learning objectives for the project.

3. Team retrospective meetings

Team retrospectives are short, informal conversations among teammates. They shouldn't last more than 15 minutes, but they should occur after every round in the peer review process so teams have a chance to reflect on their work processes together and make refinements that improve their productivity.

In what follows, we outline a three-round process in order to address some of the most frequently recurring questions about the collaborative writing process as they arise over time.

CHAPTER 5

A model for collaborative writing

Teams need to work in a sequential process at times because we all need a sense of what to do first, second, third, and so on. So starting with *empathizing*, we work from left to right in this basic model of collaborative writing.

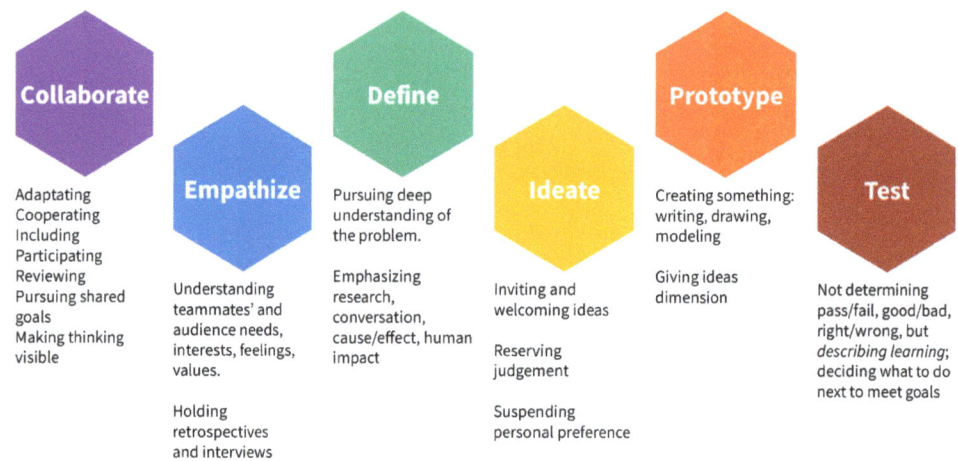

Fig. 5.5. Activities in the collaborative writing process may occur sequentially and as needed.

Do you have to do all the activities and in an exact order?

When learning the activities, you might find that doing them all and taking them in order is useful. When your whole team goes through the process together, you have the benefit of a structured sequence for a shared experience. But any of the activities can be useful at various times during the project, so don't think of the activities as something you do only once.

For example, you don't empathize with teammates only at the beginning of a writing project in order to understand how they feel about the topic or about working on the project. You might do an empathizing activity at the beginning of the project, but

CHAPTER 5

seeking to understand your teammates' feelings is an ongoing process that affects all the other aspects of the process, as symbolized by the circular and overlapping design of the process model.

The number of times you repeat your collaborative writing process or parts of it will vary depending on team dynamics, project design, and instructor preference. As with all models, the collaborative writing process model is an abstraction. We don't work inside hexagons, after all. And we don't start and stop one mental activity at a time. Instead, we move from one to the other to another and back again as we think and write.

Empathizing activities

The point of empathizing during the collaborative writing process is to keep your audience and teammates in mind while writing. Understanding and sharing the feelings of your audience and teammates helps with the writing process by helping you decide what kinds of information to include in whatever you're writing and by helping teammates work together productively.

Empathizing activities at the end of the chapter support empathy by asking you to reflect on your own feelings first. The **Interest/Confidence Conversation** focuses on your interest and confidence in pursuing specific goals as a teammate.

The **Team Charter** activity asks you and your teammates to weigh in on important aspects of the collaborative writing experience and how you envision working together.

Finally, the **Team Update Memo** activity asks you to make specific commitments during projects and to include obstacles that might affect your ability to meet those commitments.

CHAPTER 5

Interest/confidence inventory

Understanding the range of confidence and interest in key collaborative writing activities helps teams assign roles and tasks during projects and for peer review.

Sharing information about your interests and confidence helps teams avoid surprises, and knowing which teammates share a lack of confidence in one or more objectives can help identify ways that teammates can support each other.

Interest and confidence levels always vary widely, and students typically express relatively low confidence in two or more writing activities and relatively high confidence in at least one activity.

Honesty counts, and no students are expected to have high interest and high confidence in all of the activities. You can expect to see a range of responses from yourself and all of your teammates. If you find yourself rating all activities with all high scores, all low scores, or all scores of the same number on the scale, that means you might not be taking enough time to compare and contrast each of the activities.

Finally, having high interest or confidence in an objective doesn't mean you should only be assigned that objective. Similarly, having low interest or confidence doesn't mean you shouldn't be assigned to that objective. Strong teams strike a balance when sharing roles and tasks, ensuring that all teammates gain new experience, no one gets pigeon-holed, and everyone takes turns compromising.

Team charter activity

Discussing topics in the team charter activity helps teammates get acquainted with 1) each other and 2) expectations for teamwork. The team charter discussion is divided into five sections: Team name, Participation, Cooperation, Collaboration, and Working outside of class, with each designed to address the most common obstacles to team productivity.

Purpose of team charter discussions and drafting

A charter is a document that evolves with the team as individuals work and learn together. It's not a set of rigid rules, and it's never really finished. It's a work in progress. All the decisions you make are subject to review and change based on what you learn together during projects.

Focus 1: Norms for teamwork (teamwork means actively participating during meetings and contributing content while drafting or during peer review)

a. Discuss advantages of attending class meetings; discuss problems that arise when someone misses class meetings. Missing occasional meetings is reasonable but only if you notify teammates and the instructor in advance.

Advantages of participating and contributing	Problems when you don't participate or contribute

Interest/confidence inventory activity

SECTION 1

Working independently, complete the personal inventory below.

	Very low 1	2	3	4	Very high 5
My **interest** in pursuing critical thinking objectives as a member of a collaborative writing team.	◎	◎	◎	◎	◎
My **confidence** in pursuing critical thinking objectives as a member of a collaborative writing team.	◎	◎	◎	◎	◎
My **interest** in pursuing research objectives as a member of a collaborative writing team.	◎	◎	◎	◎	◎
My **confidence** in pursuing research objectives as a member of a collaborative writing team.	◎	◎	◎	◎	◎
My **interest** in pursuing genre/structure objectives as a member of a collaborative writing team.	◎	◎	◎	◎	◎
My **confidence** in pursuing genre/structure objectives as a member of a collaborative writing team.	◎	◎	◎	◎	◎
My **interest** in pursuing synthesis objectives as a member of a collaborative writing team.	◎	◎	◎	◎	◎
My **confidence** in pursuing synthesis objectives as a member of a collaborative writing team.	◎	◎	◎	◎	◎
My **interest** in pursuing review/editing objectives as a member of a collaborative writing team.	◎	◎	◎	◎	◎
My **confidence** in pursuing review/editing objectives as a member of a collaborative writing team.	◎	◎	◎	◎	◎

Interest/confidence inventory activity

After completing the personal inventory, share your results with your teammates and discuss the following questions:

- For one of the activities with your highest confidence score, how have you earned your confidence in that ability?
- Discuss one item you rated with lowest interest, briefly explaining why.
- Discuss one item you rated with lowest confidence, briefly explaining why.

SECTION 2

Compile all your teammates' ratings using the sample format in the first three rows.

Teammate name	Critical thinking	Research	Genre / structure	Synthesis	Review / editing
Jason	3/3	4/3	2/1	3/2	4/4
Gustav	2/1	5/4	3/1	2/2	3/3
Meghalee	4/3	4/4	3/2	1/1	5/4
name	I/C	I/C	I/C	I/C	I/C
name	I/C	I/C	I/C	I/C	I/C
name	I/C	I/C	I/C	I/C	I/C
name	I/C	I/C	I/C	I/C	I/C
name	I/C	I/C	I/C	I/C	I/C
name	I/C	I/C	I/C	I/C	I/C

Insert more rows as necessary.

SECTION 3

Use the following prompts to share your motivations and fears about teamwork.

a. Take turns telling stories about why you rated one of the activities highest.
b. Take turns telling stories about why you rated one of the activities lowest.

CHAPTER 5

Norms for teamwork, cont.

b. Agree on a primary and secondary way of communicating when you can't attend class or a scheduled meeting. Share contact information and time zones.

Primary	Secondary

c. How do individuals on your team prefer to contribute to team discussions? For example, some people prefer contributing during meetings. Some people prefer to take time for reflection before contributing. Both preferences (among others) must be respected. Discuss how you will ensure that all teammates weigh in before the team makes decisions.

Name	Preferences

CHAPTER 5

d. If the project requires sharing of leadership—with no single person being the team leader or spokesperson—how do all teammates feel about sharing leadership? If it's a leader-led project what potential advantages and problems do you associate with that model?

Potential advantages	Potential problems

e. What do teammates consider to be their leadership strengths? Discuss the abilities listed or others you have or want to develop.
   1. Can change as projects change.
   2. Can take on problems with a focus on finding a shared solution.
   3. Can identify strengths of the group to promote a shared objective.
   4. Can resolve conflicts without blaming.

During your discussion, take turns telling a story about a time when you used or saw someone else use one of the four abilities and explain whether you want to practice developing that ability during your project.

Focus 2: Norms for cooperation (cooperation means complying with others' requests)

a. Determine a time frame that everyone agrees on for responding to each other's messages. What's practical and reasonable?

CHAPTER 5

Norms for cooperation, cont.

b. Some teammates prefer to get their work done right away. Others prefer to wait near the deadline to complete their work. Neither preference is better than the other, but you must discuss your preferences in advance so teammates are not surprised. Make a list of pros and cons of each work preference.

	Get work done right away	Wait until close to deadline
Pros		
Cons		

c. What are some examples of respectful and disrespectful behaviors you've seen during team meetings in the past?

Respectful	Disrespectful

CHAPTER 5

d. Based on your past experience, what are examples of respectful and disrespectful negotiation during disagreements?

Respectful	Disrespectful

Focus 3: What if teammates aren't able to contribute on time?

a. Focus on your own work. Complete your contributions and peer reviews; don't wait for teammates who haven't contributed on time.

b. If your instructor has asked everyone to contribute to all sections of team-written docs, your docs shouldn't have big holes in them if one or more teammates have been unable to complete their work.

c. If you're not able to complete work on time, be in touch with teammates or your instructor as soon as possible. Everyone is late sometimes. It's not a crime. But not telling people you're going to be late in advance (or as soon as possible) contributes to panic—and it's unprofessional.

Focus 4: Norms for collaboration (collaboration means working toward shared goals). Some possible norms:

a. Proposes (but not forces) ideas, suggestions, courses of action.

b. Asks teammates for their opinion.

c. Builds on teammate ideas.

d. Offers to help teammates.

e. Invites views or opinions from team members who are not actively participating in the discussion.

CHAPTER 5

Focus 5: Norms for meeting and communicating outside of class

a. What are some of our most realistic options for meeting outside of class? When could you meet online?

b. How many of you use Google video calls, Skype, or other conferencing tools?

c. How should you share calendars?

d. What is the best way to communicate with teammates (e.g., email, text, phone call, app)?

Focus 6: Team name

All teammates provide name ideas prior to your discussion, then discuss strengths of each option before settling on a name.

Teammate	Team name suggestion

CHAPTER 5

Team update memos

Whether you're working alone or in teams, writing is very much a commitment-driven activity. At the beginning of a project you explore topics in order to find one to commit to. If you're telling a story, a key character typically commits to achieving a specific goal or outcome; if you're writing a research report, you commit to testing a hypothesis and ultimately to support a thesis. In essay writing, you commit to exploring a specific topic in order to arrive at insights. And in all cases, you commit to fulfilling basic expectations of the genre in which you're working.

In a collaborative writing project, you're also making commitments to your team—to make specific contributions, to raise questions, meet deadlines, and show up prepared to support the team's efforts. Making and meeting commitments to your team can be challenging. Many students report feelings of anxiety about measuring up to their teammates' contributions, and they report being worried about meeting deadlines. That's why it's so important to balance commitment with flexibility and good communication.

Even though you want to keep commitments to your team, you also have responsibilities to others, and that's the main reason teammates sometimes fall short of expectations. It's not because they're slackers; it's usually because you have to weigh priorities. Do you have any of the following priorities on your mind today?

> *My family is visiting this weekend.*
> *I have a big midterm coming up.*
> *I work the next three nights in a row.*
> *I have no time over the weekend to catch up.*
> *My schedule conflicts with our next meeting time.*
> *The job fair is tomorrow.*
> *My brother is seriously ill.*

CHAPTER 5

If so, you know what we mean by weighing priorities. Everyone on your team has to meet the same challenge of prioritizing, and everyone has different decisions to make. As a result, a writing process for teams has to be very different from the process you use when writing alone. For example, the process has to include time for letting teammates know what your priorities are, what obstacles you encounter, and most especially for letting teammates know when you're not able to meet commitments.

At the same time, many students report that making commitments to teammates helps them stay focused and accountable.

Working with others means sharing commitments, guessing how much time each commitment demands, learning about individual skills, interests, and experience. Sharing, guessing, and learning comprise some of the many other advantages of practicing team writing:

- Working in teams is common practice in academia, in business, and in organizations of all sizes, so practicing team writing can go right on your resume to meet requirements for communication, flexibility, and teamwork.
- Teams expose members to diverse points of view, which means when writing in teams you learn about ways other people think.
- Teams work through problems together so individuals don't have to face them alone—a serious aid to productivity.
- Teammates learn how to deal with scheduling challenges. It's not fun; it's not easy. Stuff happens. You get better at it by practicing it, not by avoiding it.
- Teammates foster emergent learning— new insights that outnumber what students can learn from an instructor alone.

CHAPTER 5

Team update memo activity

The purpose of team update memos is to clarify for yourself and for teammates the commitments you're making to the team project. At the same time, keeping track of the time you spend on projects develops your time management and planning skills.

As the example in Table 5.2 illustrates, a team update memo includes several details, many of which are subject to change. For example, in column 3 you outline what you plan to complete by the next meeting. By making your plan as specific as possible, you help the team see how the work you're doing fits in with what others are doing. If everyone adds a high level of detail, it's easy for teams to spot the potential problem of duplicated effort or the equally important issue of gaps in the plan.

Column 8 asks you to do the best you can to anticipate possible obstacles to meeting the commitments you make by the time you've committed to meet them. Many students report difficulty in making specific commitments because they don't know what's going to happen day by day, but we encourage you to make your best guess so you and your teammates have points of reference.

You will notice that entries in Table 5.2 include specific dates and times (columns 4 & 5). These quantified entries are the key to a useful update memo. In short, quantified entries have numbers assigned to them.

> *"I'm going to do research by the next meeting"* isn't quantified.
> *"I'm going to find three valid sources by Aug. 23"* is quantified.

Additional examples of quantified tasks include:

> *Read 22 pages of the assigned reading.*
> *Spend 60 minutes drafting my part of the paper.*
> *Work until I find three images for our poster presentation.*
> *Write 150 words on my topic.*

CHAPTER 5

Table 5.2. A team update memo helps you and your teammates make specific commitments to the team project. By quantifying your entries, you also develop valuable time-management skills.

Teammate name	Update for	What I'll complete	by date	and time	Time estimate (hours)	Time actual (hours)	Obstacles to finishing on time	Plans for overcoming obstacles
Amalle	Research draft	Research: find three sources	Feb 16, 2022	4:00 pm.	2	2.5	Not sure what I should do first.	Talk to teammates; check with instructor.
Amalle	Research draft	Write all major and minor parts	Feb 18, 2022	9:00 pm.	2	3.75	I might not have enough information.	Review examples of past student work for ideas about what to include.
Amalle	Research draft	Check final formatting, citations.	Feb 18, 2022	10:00 pm.	0.75	0.5	Leaving early for break.	Will have my laptop to work while traveling. Message team members if I have any questions.
Amalle	Research draft	Check spelling, consistency.	Feb 19, 2022	11:00 pm.	0.5	0.25	Friend's birthday this weekend.	Complete my tasks before Sunday: 1 hour Friday, 3 hours Saturday, 45 minutes Sunday morning.

CHAPTER 5

Defining activities

Successful collaborations often boil down to how well a team can articulate the problem at hand and keep defining it as you learn together, so problem definition—and redefinition—is another key step in the collaborative writing process.

The opposite of what we mean by defining would be for teams to briefly decide, "Okay, we're writing about topic A. Let's find some sources and see what happens." That kind of problem definition is too vague to help teams work together productively.

Instead, we're talking about *defining* as taking a little more time to take a human-centered approach to problem definition. A human-centered approach means thinking about problems and solutions in terms of the human impact that each makes on specific people or groups. So for example, instead of thinking about the problem of writing a thesis-driven essay, or a marketing plan, or a scientific report, you consider how your project addresses a need for information by specific people, including both your audience and your teammates.

Writing-centered problem definition	*Human-centered problem definition*
Writing a thesis-driven essay	Give readers a new perspective on race-based privilege to increase understanding about an important issue.
Writing a marketing plan	Show the CFO which 20% of the market accounts for 80% of revenues so they will approve a marketing budget with confidence.
Writing a scientific report	Help a busy decision maker determine the feasibility of reducing the carbon footprint of their organization.

Figure 5.6. Emphasizing specific human needs in your problem definition helps teams focus their attention on specific topics from the very beginning of the writing process.

CHAPTER 5

The purpose of defining activities for teams is to work together toward a mutual understanding of the writing project and its purpose. One of the most familiar defining activities is the drafting of a problem statement of a few sentences that capture the problem teams are focusing on and suggests the impact and urgency of the problem to be addressed.

To craft a problem statement together, start with your individual responses to the following questions:

1. Working alone, review the assignment and put the following into your own words:
    a. The purpose of the project from your instructor's point of view
    b. The audience for the completed work
    c. The needs of the audience for the content you're developing
    d. The genre or format of the final product
    e. The purpose of the final product from the audience's point of view
2. In your team, take turns presenting your responses.
3. Compare each teammate's responses to #1. a–e. with the goal of arriving at a shared understanding of the assignment.
4. Differences of opinion or interpretation are especially important to note. Take time to discuss the differences. If you're not able to reach agreement in the time you have, come back to them during team meetings.
5. Based on the information you've shared, individually draft a problem statement that captures the problem, the needs of people affected by it, and the form and purpose of the final product.
6. Repeat steps 2, 3, and 4 as needed, remembering that problem statements evolve as your team learns and writes together.

CHAPTER 5

Another important defining activity is to outline ways that teammates define the problem of meeting writing requirements together.

1. Working alone, and based on your review of project requirements, outline challenges, questions, or concerns you have about meeting project requirements together as a team.
2. In your team, take turns presenting your responses.
3. Compare each teammate'sS responses with the goal of arriving at a shared understanding of the issues all teammates have raised.

Critical thinking requirements	
Research requirements	
Genre/structure requirements	
Synthesis requirements	
Review/structure requirements	
Collaboration requirements	

Figure 5.7. Discussing key project requirements to learn how teammates interpret them helps teams identify differences that can 1) deepen understanding and 2) differences in understanding that can lead to wasted effort.

CHAPTER 5

Differences of opinion or interpretation about what the project requirements are asking you to achieve are especially important to note. Take time to discuss the differences and to keep a record of questions you have about requirements so you can raise them with your instructor. Modeled after a classic activity of design thinking and user experience design, the user story is an important tool for defining problems in human terms. A user story consists of three parts, as illustrated in Figure 5.8.

Typical user story structure:
As a < type of user >, I want < a goal > so that < some reasons >.

Example:
As a team member,
I want a shared-access work calendar,
so that I can organize team meetings.

Create your own:
As a ....
I want ....
so that ....

Figure 5.8. User stories help with problem definition by asking teams to think in specific terms of audience needs and teammate needs.

CHAPTER 5

Increment prototyping activities

What is an increment?

An increment is a small part of your project. It can be a title, a purpose statement, an image with a caption, a paragraph—any small part that you consider ready for review. Select an increment that represents a contribution you've made to the project.

Increment selection

Early in the project, you want to be sure your team is headed in the right direction, so select an increment that emphasizes your problem definition, thesis, key purpose or other content that captures your team's thinking about the overarching goals of the project.

By the midpoint, you've done quite a bit of work on your project, so the increment should reflect key ideas or important questions you have about expanding your work, sharpening your focus, or redefining the problem you're addressing.

Near the end of the project, you're preparing your work for submission and evaluation so should present an excerpt that captures the essence of your work—a key conclusion for example, or a passage that exemplifies your best work in some important way. At the end of the chapter, we discuss the increment review activity in detail.

CHAPTER 5

Prototyping practice

This activity introduces you to the design thinking process and asks you to reflect on your collaborative writing experiences with a partner.

1. Take a minute to reflect on your own collaborative writing experience. **(1 min)**
   a. What I liked about my experience (and why):

   b. What I disliked about it (and why):

2. Learn about a teammate's experience (gain empathy). Have a conversation with your partner to learn what they said in #1. **(2 mins x2)**

3. Reframe the problem in terms of needs and feelings. **(2 mins)**
   a. What does your partner need in order to have a desirable collaborative writing experience?

   b. What did you learn about your partner's feelings about collaborative writing? (Describe emotions).

CHAPTER 5

4. Prototype.

   a. What would one of your ideas look like in actual practice? **(3 mins)**

   b. Ideate (brainstorm multiple solutions). Using your findings from the interview, sketch at least five radical ways to meet your partner's needs. Don't be constrained by logic or ease at this stage. **(5 mins)**

CHAPTER 5

5. Test: Share your ideas & capture feedback.

a. What does your partner like about your ideas? Write notes directly on the sketches themselves. **(1 min)**

b. Which one is their favorite? Why? **(1 min)**

c. What would they add to your ideas? **(1 min)**

6. Reflect & generate iterative ideas. Based on your partner's feedback, sketch a revised/improved big idea. **(2 mins)**

CHAPTER 5

Increment review activities

The purpose of increment review is for teams to present a small part of the written content to the class, discuss how the increment meets project requirements, and receive feedback on their progress.

Listening to what other teams are doing—and listening to the feedback other teams receive— gives you insight into requirements and which strategies for meeting them are working, in need of rethinking, or suggest new directions as you continue working together.

What to prepare: use slides or Post-it notes or handouts, or share a link to a Google Doc with your increment highlighted: an increment may be a few sentences, a photo, an illustration, caption, outline, a paragraph, or other part of the whole. It should be large enough to illustrate achievement in each of the project requirements and no larger.

> Option 1: One increment per team. Have teammates discuss how the increment meets one project requirement each.
>
> Option 2: One increment per teammate. Have each teammate discuss how their increment meets all project requirements.

Critical thinking requirements: How does the increment

- address an audience need?
- support the purpose of the larger content of which it's a part?
- contribute to the tone of the content?
- contribute to reader trust in the content?
- help define an important concept?

CHAPTER 5

Research requirements: How does the increment meet requirements for

- accurate, credible citations?
- emphasizing human impact?
- presenting information in cause/effect form?
- making claims?
- supporting claims with valid information?

Genre/structure requirements: How does the increment

- represent content that addresses readers' needs and interests?
- address readers' values?
- represent formatting that aids users in finding information they need quickly?
- represent visual elements that meet readers' needs and interests?
- represent the requirement for descriptive captions for all figures and tables?

Synthesis requirements: How does the increment

- accurately paraphrase source information?
- represent collaborative thinking?
- includes signal phrases describing the credibility of sources?
- evaluate information to aid readers' understanding?
- represent an original conclusion you've drawn from source material?

Review and editing requirements: How does the increment

- present consistent word choice?
- support your goal of presenting information in a professional way?
- support the goal of avoiding distracting patterns of error?
- demonstrate adherence to professional publishing standards for clarity, accuracy, or consistency?
- represent collaborative editing, review, or revision?

Collaboration requirements: How does the increment represent team achievement in

- participation?
- cooperation?
- collaboration?
- working together outside of class?
- overcoming obstacles?

CHAPTER 5

Retrospective activities

Team retrospectives are short, informal conversations among teammates. They shouldn't last more than 15 minutes, but they should occur after every round in the peer review process so teams have a chance to reflect on their work processes together and make refinements that improve their productivity.

Retrospectives have three components: 1) a continuous improvement survey 2) a team retrospective meeting, and 3) a retrospective update memo. Together, the retrospective sets a direction for improving team productivity.

Continuous improvement survey

To prepare for team retrospectives, complete the following survey of teammate participation. Using the teammate continuous improvement update gives you a chance to improve team and individual productivity prior to evaluation by your instructor. The process also helps you compare understandings of key objectives for your team and reach consensus about your objectives.

At the end of the teammate continuous improvement survey, be sure to include responses to the following prompts:

- *I appreciate* . . . [note something you appreciate about the teammate's contributions]
- *My continuous communication improvement idea for you is* . . .

Teammate continuous improvement survey

Name of teammate:

Your name (provider of feedback):

This teammate . . .	Always	Usually	Sometimes	Rarely	Never	Comments
Actively participates (practices teamwork)						
Attends class meetings.	5	4	3	2	1	
Contributes to team discussions.	5	4	3	2	1	
Shares leadership.	5	4	3	2	1	
Completes a fair share of the work.	5	4	3	2	1	
Complies with others' requests (is cooperative)						
Responds to teammate messaging within the time frame agreed upon by the team.	5	4	3	2	1	
Completes tasks on time.	5	4	3	2	1	
Notifies teammates before absences or missed deadlines.	5	4	3	2	1	
Behaves respectfully toward teammates in meetings.	5	4	3	2	1	
Accepts or respectfully negotiates when others disagree with their ideas during discussions.	5	4	3	2	1	
Expresses support for teammates' opinions or ideas during discussions.	5	4	3	2	1	
Works toward shared goals (collaborates)						
Proposes (but not forces) ideas, suggestions, courses of action.	5	4	3	2	1	
Asks teammates for their opinion.						
Builds on teammate ideas.	5	4	3	2	1	
Offers to help teammates.						
Invites views or opinions from team members who are not actively participating in the discussion.	5	4	3	2	1	
Total						

CHAPTER 5

Team retrospective meeting

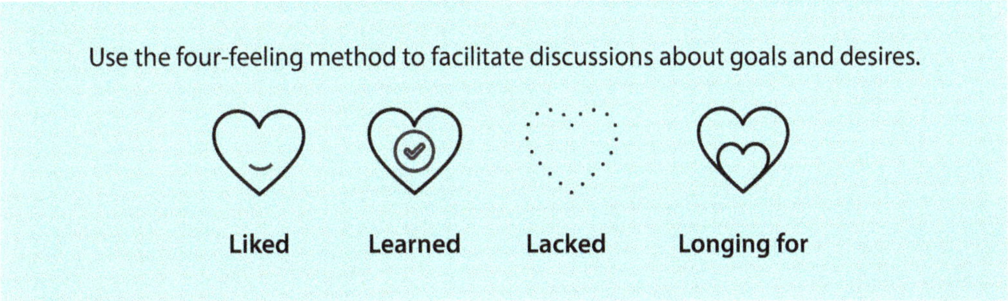

Use the four-feeling method to facilitate discussions about goals and desires.

Liked   **Learned**   **Lacked**   **Longing for**

Figure 5.9. Team retrospectives are short, informal meetings for reflecting on team performance and setting goals for improvement.

Instructions

1. Working alone, write up your responses to these three questions:

a. Thinking about a recent work period, what worked well (communication, planning, meeting deadlines, cooperating, sharing work, sharing leadership, and other activities).

b. Thinking about the same recent work period, what didn't work well. Try to focus on factual information. "I completed about 50% of what I said I would." "We were late turning in our work." Avoid blaming others. Instead, describe specific outcomes and their impact. "We underestimated how much time we needed to read and take notes on sources, so some of our claims weren't persuasive."

c. What will you do right away (individually or as a team) to improve productivity?

CHAPTER 5

2. With your team, make turns discussing your responses to #1. Make a complete list of what teammates say is working.

3. Take turns discussing responses to #2. Make a complete list of what teammates say is not working.

4. Take turns discussing reponses to #3. Make a complete list of what teammates say about changes. Discuss changes that all teammates agree to make.

5. Update your team charter so it reflects your current agreements about how you want to work together.

6. Summarize your discussion in a team retrospective memo.

CHAPTER 5

A retrospective memo

Co-authoring the update memo ensures that everyone's perspectives are included. Therefore, instead of assigning one person to summarize your retrospective meeting discussion, each teammate should contribute answers to all three questions.

> Reflect on what's working and what's not working, and make changes right away to improve inclusivity.

Teams routinely meet specifically to discuss thoughts and feelings about working together, to what extent team processes support all teammates and productivity toward project goals. Individually reflecting on what's working, what's not working, and what individuals can do right away to improve productivity is a key to successful collaboration. Capturing the range of responses to the questions in a format for sharing with teammates and the instructor gives everyone a chance to acknowledge successes, suggest improvements, and ask for support from teammates and instructor as needed.

What's working…

> *I felt included in discussions when _____.*

> *Our team is really good at _____.*

What's not working…

> *I would be more likely to contribute if _____.*

> *I could have used more time to think when we were talking about _____.*

CHAPTER 5

What we can do right away…

In order to achieve _____(goal), *we could start* _____(new process, activity, or tool) *right away.*

We could also stop doing _____ (process, activity, or tool that isn't working).

Team retrospective memo

Date:

To:

From:

CC:

Teammate attendance:

Absence:

Discussion summaries

1. What worked? In your own words, summarize your understanding of what's working for your team.

2. What didn't work? Summarize your understanding of what's not working.

3. What will you as an individual do differently right away to improve productivity for your team?

Figure 5.10. The retrospective memo gives teammates a chance to reflect on team productivity and add their perspectives to one shared document.

CHAPTER 5

Midpoint changes

As teams deepen their understanding of each other and of project requirements, you begin to see changes in your team at the same time as you narrow the scope of your efforts. During this stage, a lot of learning takes place, and you want to remain flexible and open to new ideas and changing strategies.

Empathizing with teammates: continue learning how teammates feel about the project and working on the team.

Your understanding of how readers and teammates feel about your topic may evolve throughout the project. By the midpoint, your own feelings might change—you might feel frustrated at times, feeling that if you had only known something earlier, you could have saved time. It's usually more productive to think of what you learn along the way as a sign of progress than as a sign of error or wasted time. Apply what you learned to new ways of thinking about the project and improving how you work together as a team.

Defining: teams typically continue redefining the problem over time. You're also redefining what it means to write collaboratively, and you're redefining your understanding of what the problem you're exploring actually is. Questions often arise about how to define or redefine the problem you're writing about, and that's another important sign of progress. Assumptions—spoken or unspoken—turn out to be invalid, for example. That's a normal part of the collaborative process and a sign that you're learning together.

Prototyping: at the beginning of the project, you thought about the topic of your work broadly and you initially defined the problem, why it's worth exploring, and how it might be addressed. By now several problems related to the initial problem have revealed themselves. Taking time to brainstorm possible solutions to the new problems you're facing helps to ensure that you're all working together with a shared understanding of the problems. Agree to take a direction that might work and visualize the direction in a prototype.

CHAPTER 5

Testing: present your prototype in order to get feedback so you can refine the direction. Briefly present an increment to the class, explaining how it represents achievement in addressing new problems that are related to the initial problem you set out to address.

Team retrospective: reflect on what's going well, specifically with respect to meeting project objectives. What isn't going well, and what changes can individuals and the whole team make right away to improve productivity?

Project review: The closer you are to the deadline, the more you focus on the written work and final refinements. Now, instead of increment review, you're reviewing the entire work and strategically refining it before submitting it to your instructor.

During project review, each teammate takes one role and makes suggestions for meeting specific project requirements:

- **Critical thinking** means paying attention to audience, purpose, tone, definition, counter-argument, author and source credibility, and academic honesty.
- **Research** means paying attention to research questions, hypotheses, human impact, cause/effect, methods, results, and discussion.
- **Genre/structure** means paying attention to required content and organization.
- **Synthesis** means paying attention to claims, signal phrases, paraphrasing, citations, evaluation and interpretation of course content, readings, and sources.
- **Review/editing** means being mindful of project requirements and adding notes that will help your teammates achieve goals of the project.
- **Collaboration** means paying attention to teamwork, cooperation, communication, shared leadership, and conflict resolution.

CHAPTER 5

Differing work flows

Teams typically include members whose work habits differ dramatically and those differences can become more prominent midway through the project. One of the most common differences is teammates' approaches to deadlines. Some people are deadline driven—they prioritize their work for the project and other coursework by when it's due. Others want to get work off of their plates as soon as possible after it's assigned. Both approaches have advantages and disadvantages. Off-the-platers develop content right away, which gives the team momentum, makes thinking visible, and sets a direction. On the other hand, work produced right away might require revision based on new learning. Teammates who are deadline driven have the advantage of more time to include new learning. At the same time, some teammates may become anxious while waiting for others to contribute close to the deadline. Neither preference is right or wrong. One of the best ways to prevent problems associated with different work styles is to keep a shared document updated with commitments, obstacles, and progress.

Revisiting communication ground rules

While teammates' working styles vary significantly, teams can hold everyone to the same communication guidelines, preferably ones that teams create together. Revisiting guidelines you established at the beginning of the project can help teams stay productive by reminding teammates of important agreements and by giving teams a chance to revise guidelines as needed. Ground rules should make clear, for example, that being deadline driven doesn't mean disappearing from group discussions until the last minute and that working in advance doesn't mean outlining a rigid time frame for the whole team to follow.

Teammates who like to work in advance should let their teammates know of their preference without expecting everyone to work the same way. Teammates who are deadline driven should let teammates know of their preference without expecting everyone else to slow down. Making preferences clear, schedules clear, and commitments as accurate as possible are important steps in supporting team productivity.

CHAPTER 5

Awareness of different work habits only goes so far, and even the best project plan has dependencies. Because working close to deadlines is effective for some teammates and working ahead works for others, few are going to change their habits significantly. Therefore teammates should expect to receive reminders and to accept the reminders courteously. The reminders should be written in a professional tone and should not suggest that anyone is doing something wrong unless a teammate has missed a deadline without having informed teammates in advance. Teammates should acknowledge receipt of reminders at the very least and provide updates on progress with a revised schedule for completing their work.

Missing deadlines is not as big a problem as not warning teammates in advance about missing them. Teammates who fear they're going to be labeled slackers if they miss a deadline are less likely to broadcast the fact than teammates who trust they won't be judged. When a teammate is going to miss a deadline, the most important information is not about why. The most important information is about when the team can expect to see the work.

Slacking really is slacking when a teammate makes a commitment, makes it visible, includes measurable goals and a due date and then 1) doesn't deliver, and 2) hasn't notified teammates in advance.

Paying attention to the true complexities of writing and collaboration—and talking about them with teammates—helps teams identify the true causes for lapses in productivity, which is a necessary step in the process of improving team performance.

Someone has taken over

Collaboration stops when one or more people decide they need to take over the project. If someone does take over, it usually has a negative impact on the team. Some teammates may feel discouraged from continuing to work on the project, while others may get lost because they're not engaged and can't get up to speed because someone else has written so much of the work.

CHAPTER 5

Teammates who feel like they want to take over should discuss their concerns about team productivity with teammates. Teams should also clarify with the instructor what their expectations are to determine how grading works for the group project. If the instructor only grades individuals by the contributions they make to the team-written document, contributors' grades wouldn't suffer if one or more teammates doesn't make sufficient contributions. Similarly, if someone does all the work, others don't have the opportunity to contribute without being repetitive.

Sitting back while others do all the work

Letting others do the work for reasons other than illness or other emergency is the classic example of slacking. In most cases, it's not true that students who don't write as much as others are slacking. Instead, they have less experience or are facing obstacles that other teammates are not.

But if you're in a course that includes a group project and the course is a low priority for you, you owe it to yourself and your teammates to let them know. Doing so serves the team by helping to manage expectations; it helps you by taking pressure off. It's not like you're going to fool anyone by failing to say right up front that you're not fully invested in the course. Signs that you're giving a course low priority include poor attendance, habitually late work, poor communication, and other unmet requirements. Instructors who take attendance and monitor individual contributions to team projects easily spot teammates who are not invested.

Collaborative writing projects are opportunities to share leadership by adopting an attitude and practice of supporting team productivity, and that attitude applies both to people who are inclined to take up the slack for others and to those who are inclined to sit back and take credit for other teammates' work.

Shared leadership includes patience with teammates whose work habits are different from your own. Some people finish work at the last minute; others get their work done ahead of time. Both work styles have advantages and disadvantages.

Do your fair share, and no more. Doing someone else's work for them can really backfire. For one, it creates more work for you. As importantly, it can make others

CHAPTER 5

feel discouraged, as if you don't want them to contribute or don't believe they have something valuable to add.

In other words, "picking up the slack" is not always a sign of initiative or leadership. An attitude and practice of supporting team productivity means sending a courteous reminder and using team meetings and peer review to support all teammates.

Similarly, leaving the work to everyone else is not fair to teammates or to yourself. Taking credit for others' work is dishonest, and while it can be tempting to let others do the studying and writing, in the end you're wasting the learning opportunity afforded by the project. Thanks to cloud-based writing tools, instructors are able to see who made entries on shared documents, so in most cases it's obvious who has and has not contributed.

Giving and receiving negative feedback

Constructive feedback is about identifying strengths and making suggestions for improvement. Overly negative feedback or the use of a harshly critical tone can discourage teammates from taking risks or even contributing. That's why taking time to discuss peer feedback during team meetings is a good practice after a round of peer review.

To avoid giving overly negative feedback when commenting on teammates' work, look for high achievement to comment on as well as work that needs improvement. Looking for high achievement gives you and teammates a point of reference. "This paragraph isn't as clear as the one above because it doesn't include an example. You could add an example to make this paragraph as good as the previous one" lets the teammate know what they're capable of while providing a guide to achieving greater consistency.

When instructors assign specific tasks to each peer reviewer, you have the advantage of knowing where to focus your attention. Referring to specific requirements in your comments is more helpful than generic or vague comments like leaving just a question mark or writing "unclear" or other one-word notes.

CHAPTER 5

Labeling your comments with the name of the requirement you're addressing helps remind you and teammates of key requirements. For you, labeling comments also helps ensure you're providing relevant feedback. For teammates, labels help everyone identify areas of strengths and opportunities for improvement that have the highest priority because they're based on specific project requirements.

Looking ahead

As you pursue collaborative writing goals, questions arise about how to respond to problems or overcome obstacles. The final chapter takes you to next-level collaboration by using strategic ways to address team obstacles.

CHAPTER 6

NEXT-LEVEL COLLABORATION

GUIDING QUESTIONS

- How can teams use what they learn during projects to improve their writing process?
- How do empathy and problem definition help teams avoid or address challenges of team writing?

CHAPTER 6

Many books might call this chapter *Troubleshooting* or *Conflict resolution*, but we call it *Next-level collaboration* because teams advance a level every time they encounter a problem and address it head-on. Teams build trust and achieve higher productivity when they solve problems together, so referring to problems as trouble or conflict seems inaccurate.

Like peer review, research, and critical thinking, next-level collaboration requires skills that only improve with practice. We have found that a people-centered process for problem solving such as design thinking is especially effective for collaborative writing teams. Because of its emphasis on empathy and problem definition, the design thinking process takes into account the writers on the team and the problem you're addressing together.

Taking time to understand what teammates are thinking and feeling about the problem is key to defining what the problem is. This process begins with empathizing with the experience of the team to get insights for how each teammate feels about working together. This includes frustrations as well as delight. After learning about each member's feeling and desires for the team, define what it is that can be addressed in order to enhance team relationships. In defining specific problems, be sure to focus on the requirements of the project. Here are examples of effective and ineffective problem definition:

> Ineffective: *We are not meeting deadlines because Sam always works at the last minute.*

> Effective: *We did not meet the deadline for the project proposal because our current writing workflow conflicts with the scheduling needs of some members. We need to review our check-in time and methods.*

Once the team agrees on the defined problem(s), you may exercise brainstorming to ideate different ways of approaching the problem. Design thinking favors radical yet viable solutions. This means you and your teammates should "dream big" but keep grounded in the requirements of the collaborative project. Find a time for your team to generate a few big ideas to troubleshoot the problem, then, select one or a combination of few ideas to adopt for the troubleshooting. Prototype the adopted solution by crafting new team charters, new project timeline, or even new roles

CHAPTER 6

for members. Finally, build in a time to check on the effectiveness of the solution. Conduct peer reviews using the project requirements to test if your solution has helped create better collaboration for the team.

Next-level basics

The most common problems that occur during team writing projects fall into a handful of categories. We'll look at each one from two perspectives in order to illustrate how different teammates might perceive the same problem.

- Lack of cooperation
- Control vs leadership
- Different writing styles
- Language barriers
- Unequal contributions
- Problems related to time
- Dealing with stress
- Stereotyping

Lack of cooperation

Perspective A	Perspective B
I wrote to my teammates but they never responded.	They copied everyone on the team so I thought someone else would respond.
She didn't let us know that she wouldn't be in class.	With so much going on, I forgot to let them know I wouldn't be there. The nasty email after didn't exactly make me want to let them know next time.
When I asked if anyone wanted to add anything, they didn't speak up.	My English isn't as good as my teammates' and they get impatient when I talk.

If you send messages to more that one teammate at a time, recipients might assume that someone else will respond. A good way to address that problem is to target your messages and ask specific teammates for a response.

CHAPTER 6

If a teammate doesn't honor a team agreement, such as notifying teammates of an absence in advance, how you respond to the absence matters as much as the absence. Cooperation always goes both ways, so keeping frustration or anger out of follow-up messages is a good idea.

Some teammates might repeatedly fail to honor team agreements, which means they haven't made cooperation a priority. Your options include keeping notes about the teammate's non-responsiveness, doing peer evaluations in which you give the teammate low cooperation marks, and providing factual information to your instructor about the teammate's lack of cooperation.

Sometimes body language or a look or gesture might make some teammates feel uncomfortable contributing to projects.

Unequal contributions

Perspective A	Perspective B
They get credit for my work.	They made decisions without asking me.
I couldn't finish my work because they didn't finish theirs.	They don't understand that I have to work on weekends.
I took on about 90% of the workload.	It's their way or the highway.

Teams should discuss what equal contributions are. If you're going by word count, that's easy to track. Instructors typically provide minimum requirements for projects, and if they include minimums per teammate, everyone knows what the expectations are.

If word counts are by project instead of by teammate, you'll have to divide the word count by the number of team members to arrive at a minimum requirement per teammate.

CHAPTER 6

Contributions also occur during meetings, so showing up, sharing ideas, and raising questions are all ways teammates can contribute to projects, although those contributions can be harder to measure and evaluate.

When you are frequently absent from class or meetings, everyone notices, and even if your word count is good, your credibility among teammates will fall if you don't show up. Typically the value of your writing goes down, too, because if you miss class you likely miss important information about what content to include or how to include it.

Our recommendation is for instructors to grade only individual contributions to a project, so if one person doesn't complete their fair share of work, only that person's grade is affected. If an instructor gives one team grade to all teammates and one or more teammates is not contributing, notify your instructor.

"Weak" contributions

In cases when teammates do contribute to a project but not everyone agrees that the contributions are positive, it's time to talk about the project requirements. You don't want to sound harsh or judgmental, so raising questions about requirements instead of others' abilities is a good practice.

In some cases, a teammate might have a different understanding of what requirements are asking for, and those differences are worth discussing. In some cases a teammate might have an incorrect understanding of what the requirements are asking for, and a discussion can advance their learning.

When you're not sure whether a teammate's contribution adds value to the project, you can ask questions like these:

> "Say a little bit about how you see [this content] addressing one of the project requirements."

> "Which requirement does [this content] meet?"

> "I see where you addressed the first part of the requirement but not the second part."

CHAPTER 6

What are your team norms for editing when a teammate has less experience with English than others and their written language isn't clear? Some options include highlighting words or phrasing and raising questions using the comments function; using the suggesting or track changes function to insert suggested edits and let the author decide whether to accept or reject the suggestions.

Control vs leadership

Perspective A	Perspective B
I took charge but ended up having to do the most work.	Someone else took over, so I just gave up.
Teammates don't follow instructions.	They wouldn't stop bossing everyone around.
They never say anything.	They don't give me time to say anything.

To some people, leadership means taking charge and telling everyone what to do. For others, leadership means ensuring that all people have a say in the direction of projects. We've found that to take full advantage of the diversity of ideas in teams, making an effort to ensure that all teammates contribute the same is the fairest and most rewarding form of leadership in writing teams. We don't mean counting words and setting timers to ensure everyone speaks exactly the same amount of time during meetings and contributes exactly the same number of words to drafts. We mean all teammates who uphold the value of roughly equal contributions from everyone by inviting and reminding others can help the team reach its full potential.

CHAPTER 6

Issues related to time

Perspective A	Perspective B
We can never agree on a time to meet.	If we could just check in with each other for fifteen minutes, it would make a difference.
My team works efficiently and always finishes work on time. I knew that I could trust my team to finish the project, even if the work was not completed until the day it was due.	Teammate would only put effort in at the last second possible.
I have to make my other projects a priority because they're in my major.	I'm making this project a priority because it's in my major.

Time management is a challenge for everyone and expecting all teammates to be able to meet regularly outside of class is probably not realistic. Meeting online briefly, however, can make a big difference in a team's productivity when teammates review deadlines and confirm which high-priority tasks to work on next. Updates about progress are helpful, too, and need not take a long time to discuss.

Keeping a team update memo current lets teammates know when they can expect work from you.

CHAPTER 6

Different writing styles

Perspective A	Perspective B
It's hard to combine different voices.	Others changed my wording.
Not all contributions work.	What I contributed got deleted.
I had to edit what others wrote.	I'm embarrassed about my grammar.

In many respects, writing is a very personal activity and teammates will have a variety of feelings about their writing styles and teammates' responses to them. Discussing and honoring teammate preferences for changing, deleting, or moving content helps build trust. Until you know your teammates' preferences, a good policy is to make suggestions or ask questions about content instead of changing it in any way.

Dealing with stress

Perspective A	Perspective B
I hope I'm not the worst writer.	I hope I'm not the best writer.
I'm afraid my teammates will reject my ideas.	I'm afraid my teammates won't share their ideas.
My grandfather is very ill. It's hard to focus on the project.	My boss dropped a huge project on me. There goes my writing time.

You can assume that everyone on your team is dealing with one kind of stress or another, so the presence of stress is not by itself a cause of poor teamwork. Rather,

CHAPTER 6

it's the feeling that it's never okay to talk about being stressed that causes problems. One difference between high-performing teams and lower-performing teams, Google researchers found, is that high-performing teams are made up of more people who were sensitive to others' stress and make it okay to talk about how they're feeling. That sensitivity is another reason we chose to model the collaborative writing process after design thinking—because its first step is empathy.

Brief check-ins to acknowledge what teammates are dealing with before getting to work is therefore part of a strong team environment for collaboration.

Stereotyping

Perspective A	Perspective B
They never say anything, so I assume they don't have any ideas.	My group seems to agree with whoever talks first. As if the most talkative person has the best ideas.
They assumed I'd never done research before, and that hurt.	I'm the only female so they always ask me to take notes.
Just because I have to travel for sports doesn't mean I'm not committed to the project.	Yes, I'm tall and Black. No, I don't play basketball.

Stereotyping and bias are closely related reactions that are grounded in conscious and unconscious ideas about people. When we make assumptions about someone's aptitude or interests based on physical appearance, race, gender, clothing, gender identity, or disability, for example, we're stereotyping.

Bias might show up as an assumption about people having expertise or an interest in issues related to their race, gender identity, ethnicity, or nationality.

CHAPTER 6

Being sensitive to bias and stereotyping is a start. If you feel uncomfortable with words or behaviors in the group, others are too, so naming the feeling is one way of redirecting the conversation.

> "I'm not comfortable with that."

> "I'm concerned about the feelings of everyone in the group, so we need to talk about what you're saying."

Redirecting attention to group norms or broader guidelines is also effective.

> "Let's stop a second and talk about norms for group discussions."

> "The institution/college/department/syllabus has some guidelines for group discussions we need to review."

Next-level FAQs

My teammates don't respond when I ask them to complete their work. What should I do?

- Has your team agreed that it's your job to ask them to complete their work? If so, remind them of that, and ask once for them to contribute.
- If your team hasn't agreed that it's your job to ask them to contribute, try reframing the situation. Instead of asking others to do their work, keep teammates up to date about the work you have completed, and leave it at that.
- Cooperation is an important professional value, so responding to teammates' correspondence should be an expectation for all teams. Ignoring questions or requests is unprofessional.

CHAPTER 6

A teammate sends too many messages/questions/demands. What should I do?

- Discuss team norms for communicating. Does the team agree that it's okay for someone to send reminders? Should teammates send questions as soon as they come up or save them for team meetings?
- Discuss the problem of sending questions to more than one teammate at a time. Establish a norm that all teammates will respond when that happens. Or, establish a norm that all questions should be targeted to specific teammates.

Some teammates do their work right away and expect me to do that too, but I prefer to complete work by order of due date. My teammates wait until the last minute to do their work. What should I do?

- Have a team conversation about work styles. How many teammates prefer to do work far in advance of deadlines; how many work closer to deadlines? Both styles have advantages and disadvantages. Teammates should make their style preference clear without demanding change from others.
- Remind teammates to keep their update memos current.
- Take turns making compromises to your preferred work styles. Compromising can be a good way to increase productivity. Too much compromise, and expecting compromise from the same teammate(s) too often, can lead to lower quality, lower productivity, and feelings of alienation.

Our team needs to work on communication, but we don't know what to do.

- The team charter includes a discussion topic about favored apps for communication. Have a talk about apps and teammates' familiarity with each. Don't assume all teammates have access to the same tools or quality of internet service, so find means that are available to all teammates.
- With teammates so busy with other courses and work and friends and family, teams may have to discuss communication issues several times before teams see change. Check in with each other and revisit team norms frequently. Kind reminders about norms can be effective.

CHAPTER 6

One teammate rarely comes to class. How might we still collaborate?

- Attendance is an intractable problem for collaborative writing teams and instructors. While few alternatives to face-to-face meetings can achieve the goals of productive collaboration—reaching consensus, coordinating tasks, defining problems, agreeing on solutions, to name a few—absenteeism is inevitable, and teams can be productive in spite of it.
- Evaluating individual performance on the basis of collaboration, cooperation, and participation helps bring issues out in the open.
- Maintaining your team update memo helps to clarify what all teammates are working on, so teammates who don't attend class should keep their teammates updated on progress.
- Norms in your team charter for collaboration, cooperation, and participation should spell out team expectations.
- Add the following norms to your team charter and discuss them. When you have to miss a class session or team meeting, the following norms apply:
    1. All teammates should be aware of the team's shared goals and prioritize their work to pursue them.
    2. All teammates should honor the team charter and communication norms.
    3. All teammates should initiate contact with teammates, initiate discussions, and avoid being reactive, in catch-up mode.

I have to do all the work for the group while some people do nothing. How should I address this?

- It's rare to hear such a comment in projects designed for interdependent work in which all teammates are expected to contribute to all major parts of a project and are graded only on the work they contribute. When individuals are graded only on their own contributions, doing nothing is not an option.
- "Having" to do more than a fair share is more common in projects in which the instructor gives a team grade. In those cases, some teammates feel anxious and do more work than they should because they fear others won't pull their weight. That approach can negatively affect others by discouraging

CHAPTER 6

them from contributing ("They did everything already") or making them feel bullied.
- To address problems arising from one or more persons taking on too much responsibility, review the project guidelines for interdependent work. Clarify what each teammate will contribute to each main section of the project, and update team communications to reflect the understanding.

My teammate keeps nagging me about where my work is. Do I really have to respond to all their emails and texts?

- Keeping your update memos current helps teammates keep track of everyone's progress and minimizes questions about when you plan to complete your work. Responding once that your memo is up to date is reasonable.
- Not responding to any texts or emails about your progress can make teammates anxious, so responding at least once—or better yet, letting teammates know in advance that something has come up, that you'll be out of touch for awhile, or that you're traveling, and so on—is a very helpful courtesy.

We have a lot of problems with technology. What should we do?

- In exchange for the advantages that technologies offer, they first demand our patience. Taking a long view—that trial and error are part of the learning process, that teammates have widely varying experience with apps, that what's old to some teammates is new to others—helps with patience and keeps anxiety in check.
- For online meetings, open the app 5-10 minutes before the meeting starts. Test your mic and camera.
- Discuss teammate familiarity with apps—avoid assuming everyone has the same access to devices, internet service, and apps.
- Discuss norms for response times.
- Adapt as needed.

CHAPTER 6

Mistakes to avoid if you make decisions on your own as a team

In essays from 295 students in college writing courses over a four-year period, students wrote about positive and negative experiences they had while working in collaborative writing teams. Their insights have guided many an assignment redesign in our courses and they've culminated in the following list of collaborative writing do's and don'ts.

> Do require all teammates to contribute to all key parts of the project
> *Don't assign sections to individual teammates*
>
> Do include everyone
> *Don't form cliques*
>
> Do get support
> *Don't try to figure out the challenges of team writing on your own*
>
> Do take advantage of strength in numbers
> *Don't forget about the value of peer review*

Do require all teammates to contribute to all key parts of the project
Don't assign sections to individual teammates

While dividing projects into sections and assigning one teammate to each section might seem logical, it's usually not a productive way to divide the work. If you assign one teammate to, for example, write the introduction, one to write part A, another to write part B, and another to write the conclusion, that probably means someone has to wait for someone else to do their work.

When teams divide tasks by section, they've handcuffed themselves with dependencies. It's hard to write an introduction until you have something to introduce, for example. It's hard to write a conclusion until the parts are finished. With so much waiting occurring, learning and productivity suffer.

To be productive, the team needs a shared understanding of what the parts are and how the parts of the whole fit together, so having all teammates contribute to

CHAPTER 6

all parts of the whole is a good alternative to dividing by section. Dividing work by section can undermine shared understanding because in too many cases, teammates who aren't in charge of part A pay too little attention to the development of part A. What's in part A and how it's related to part B becomes apparent eventually but often comes late in the process as the deadline nears.

There's a better way. When you require all teammates to leave fingerprints on each major section of the project, each teammate has a stake in contributing something of value throughout the work. As importantly, having a shared responsibility for the entire project motivates students to understand what their teammates are doing and writing. The interrelatedness of the sections becomes apparent early on as each teammate considers how to make their contributions to each section.

Do include everyone
Don't form cliques

One of the surest ways to create more work for yourself is to create resentment and alienate teammates. Few people would intentionally set out to do that, yet sometimes that happens unintentionally. How? Several actions that may seem like common sense actually make some teammates feel dismissed or left out.

Voting for example. Voting has a way of creating winners and losers, and if the same teammate(s) get voted down all the time, they are likely to stop contributing to discussions. An alternative to counting how many people favor ideas, a more collaborative approach is to determine how many different ideas teammates have.

All ideas are not equally valid or productive, so having some way to determine which direction to take is a must. Instead of taking a vote based on personal preferences, use criteria based on project requirements.

Instead of rushing to reach consensus, which suggests looking for similarities among ideas, look for differences, variances, divergences. Sometimes differences of opinion are based on a person's disciplinary orientation to a topic; sometimes differences are based on teammate identities.

CHAPTER 6

Do get support
Don't try to figure out the challenges of team writing on your own

Since you're part of a team, your teammates are a great learning resource. If you have a question about your project, some of your teammates likely have some too, so asking questions is a simple but powerful way to collaborate.

> "While doing the research for project two, I had to consult with my teammates several times and get help from them. That was the nice thing about working in a team, it forced me to communicate and ask questions, which helped me to learn much more, even if I thought I was pestering people too much. Overall it was a great learning experience for me."

> "I was expressing my issues to Matt and Parker. Both members added that they were having similar issues and we worked out our problems together."

> "My confidence was reinforced when Owen and I were working together on the Feasibility Report. As we worked together, I found myself finding little issues that I likely would have overlooked before this class. Still lacking confidence, I would bounce ideas off Owen and a majority of the time I was on the right track. Similar situations with other teammates reinforced that I had made some major improvements in both structure and synthesis."

Do take advantage of strength in numbers
Don't forget about the value of peer review

Thinking too narrowly about the purpose of peer review can undermine its potential. Instructors often assign peer review in order to give students feedback on their written work. Peer review in this respect leads to improved writing. Here's what students say is the value of peer review during team writing projects:

> "My teammates made team writing very enjoyable since each of us made quality comments on our work in order to come up with the best product we could."

CHAPTER 6

> "I appreciated the feedback I received from my teammates during peer review. By reviewing other students' documents, I was able to assess my own progress and incorporate their ideas into my work."

While peer review does indeed lead to improvements in the written product, doing peer review also improves your learning. Particularly, peer review has a way of changing reviewers' perceptions of your writing requirements:

> "Organization is one of my personal strengths throughout my life, so being able to utilize that skill within my peer review in a way that I hadn't experienced before was very refreshing. I initially thought this role was a bit of a "filler" role, as genre and structure can both be very vague terms. However, through project two, I very quickly found out that it was quite the opposite. Simply making sure that the essay was following the guidelines/prompt, and ensuring that each teammate was contributing to each section was highly important."

Peer review can help with the need to engage students online while supporting key learning objectives:

> "I also really appreciated how my group was willing to help each other whenever any of us had a question or someone felt like they were not completing their peer review portion correctly. For example, I can think of a time when we were in our Zoom breakout room and one of my group members was revising the genre/structure and asked for group feedback. After asking for feedback we were able to recognize that this group member was correcting the captions and in-text citations wrong. We were able to fix this mistake as a group and we all gained knowledge in how to use genre and structure correctly."

CHAPTER 6

Look for these red flags in your group and talk about them as soon as they occur

Going too fast

Your group values decision making over processing, failing to account for critical information and consider multiple perspectives. What does going too fast look like?

- Saying yes to the first suggestion.
- Someone says, "Let's talk about that later" and it turns into never.
- Trying to solve a problem before you've defined the problem.

   Solutions include taking time to formulate suggestions, to keep track of discussion topics, and to empathize with teammates so you can define the problem before you try to solve it.

Silence

Differences of opinion turn into stubbornness, and deliberation stops. Uncertainty turns into silence. Everyone goes their own way. Teammates aren't sure what to do but don't know how to talk about it. If any of those red flags starts flying, say something right away or contact your instructor. The clock is ticking. Some teams don't gel as quickly as others, so if your team goes silent, you need to act.

Passive inaction

Team agrees on a direction without deliberation. Nobody is really invested. Productivity falls.

   Solutions

   Try *speed teaming*. Like speed networking, the idea is to spend a few minutes with someone to get acquainted and then to move on to get acquainted with someone else. The goal is to look for points of common interest.

CHAPTER 6

- How do you feel about being on a collaborative writing team?
- What's your idea of a really good learning experience?
- Do you prefer to do your homework right away or do you wait until near the deadline?
- If you have a major, why did you choose it?
- Where's the best place to eat before or after class?
- Do you study more in the morning or afternoon or at night?
- How many hours per week do you work at a job and where do you work?
- What do you wish the instructor would do to help the team work better together?
- What do you think the team could do to work better together?

Hold a team retrospective meeting

Retrospectives have three components: 1) a continuous improvement survey 2) a team retrospective meeting, and 3) a retrospective update memo. Together, the retrospective sets a direction for improving team productivity. See chapter 5 for details.

Silencing

A teammate tries to contribute but gets shut down. Shutting a teammate down can be done verbally or nonverbally and it can happen on purpose or unintentionally. Either way, when you sense that someone feels silenced or not listened to, making a little extra effort to invite their opinions can help a lot. During conversations, also ask others to hold off on second comments until everyone has a chance to weigh in once.

REFERENCES

African American & African Studies. (2010). University of Minnesota Writing Plan. https://bit.ly/3u0dVcN

Brewer, J.D., & Klein, S., (2006). Type of positive interdependence and affiliation motive in an asynchronous, collaborative learning environment. *Educational Technology Research and Development, 54*(4), 331–354.

Bruffee, K. (1993). *Collaborative learning: Higher education, independence, and the authority of knowledge*. The Johns Hopkins University Press.

Brumberger, E., & Lauer, C. (2015). The evolution of technical communication: An analysis of industry job postings. *Technical Communication, 62*(4), 224–243.

Carr, P.B. & Walton, G.M. (2014). Cues of working together fuel intrinsic motivation. *Journal of Experimental Social Psychology, 53*, 169–184.

College of Biological Sciences. (2017). University of Minnesota Writing Plan. https://bit.ly/3rXE1v0

Communication Studies. (2019). Learning objectives. University of Minnesota. http://bit.ly/3u2ED4l

Deloitte. (2018). The rise of the social enterprise. *Deloitte global human capital trends*. Deloitte Insights. https://bit.ly/3avlgcF

DeSilver, D. (2014). Who makes minimum wage? Pew Research Center. https://pewrsr.ch/3NivvSZ

Dicks, S. (2013). How can technical communicators manage projects? In J. Johnson-Eilola & S. Selber (Eds.), *Solving problems in technical communication* (pp. 310–335). The University of Chicago Press.

Ede L. & Lunsford A. (1990). *Singular texts/plural authors: Perspectives on collaborative authoring*. Southern Illinois University Press.

Flaherty, S. C. & Sadler, L. S. (2011). A review of attachment theory in the context of adolescent parenting. *Journal of Pediatric Health Care, 25*(2), 114–121. https://doi.org/10.1016/j.pedhc.2010.02.005

REFERENCES

Johnson, D. W., Johnson, R. T., & Smith, K. A. (2007). The state of cooperative learning In postsecondary and professional settings. *Educational Psychology Review, 19*, 15–29.

Kirsch, D.J., Pinder-Amaker, S.L., Morse, C. et al. (2014). Population-based initiatives in college mental health: Students helping students to overcome obstacles. *Current Psychiatry Reports, 16*(12), 525. https://doi-org.ezp1.lib.umn.edu/10.1007/s11920-014-0525-1

Moses, J. (2015). Agile writing: A project management approach to learning. *International Journal of Sociotechnology and Knowledge Development, 7*(2), 1–13.

Mulligan, C. (2009, Nov. 18). The minimum wage and teenage jobs. *The New York Times.* https://nyti.ms/36vnCsv

Pope-Ruark, R. (2012). We scrum every day: using scrum project management framework for group projects. *College Teaching, 60*(4), 164–169.

Pope-Ruark, R. (2015). Introducing agile project management strategies in technical and professional communication courses. *Journal of Business and Technical Communication, 29*(1), 112–133.

Rousu, M. (2014, Apr. 7). Let's eliminate the minimum wage for teenagers. *Forbes.* https://bit.ly/37W2P1H

Team 3. (2021). *A report on the feasibility of achieving a livable wage in Minnesota by increasing the minimum wage.* [Unpublished student report].

Team 4-8. (2021). *Feasibility report on improving mental health resources for students at the University of Minnesota–Twin Cities.* [Unpublished student report].

Team C. (2016). *How safe is your profile?* [Unpublished student report].

Theater Arts and Dance. (2015). University of Minnesota Writing Plan. https://bit.ly/3pkGj5K

Writing Enriched Curriculum Program. (2011–2019). University of Minnesota. Writing Plans. http://bit.ly/3dgjwWp

GLOSSARY

Audience
The people who need to use, read, or view the content you develop.

Assessment
A process for determining and describing how thoroughly you have met project requirements.

- Individual grades represent assessment of individual achievement.
- Team grades represent assessment of team interdependence.

Collaborative writing
Structured activities for teammates in interdependent writing roles that complement course-specific learning objectives.

Collaborative writing tasks
Specific activities assigned to teammates in writing roles. The tasks are designed to help you meet course learning objectives.

Collaborative writing process
Activities and goals designed specifically for collaborative writing teams.

1. Collaborating: Continuously improving your skills for adaptability, inclusivity, and teamwork.
2. Empathizing: understanding the feelings of others.
3. Defining: arriving at shared meanings.
4. Ideating: brainstorming a lot of ideas.
5. Prototyping: turning ideas into something tangible.
6. Testing: conducting various reviews for assessment purposes
   - Team review: explaining how content examples meet project requirements.
   - Team update meetings: short meetings about what you've completed, what you plan to complete by the next meeting, what obstacles you encounter, and how you plan to overcome the obstacles
   - Team retrospective: a discussion about what's working for the team, what's not working, and how to make changes right away to improve productivity.

GLOSSARY

Collaborative writing environment
Tangible and intangible conditions that support productive collaboration.

- Transparency: sharing thoughts and feelings with others.
- Review: discussing ideas from multiple points of view.
- Adaptation: changing based on learning.

Content
Written or visual information created or gathered for inclusion in projects.

Continuous improvement updates
Teammate feedback on your achievements specifically with regard to cooperation and collaboration.

Cooperation
Achievement in responding to others' requests during projects.

Draft
Preliminary version of content subject to review by teammates and instructor.

Drafting
Putting words and visual content down on "the page" while developing a preliminary version of content.

Evaluation
Determining the value of content and performance.

Genre
A category or type of document distinguished by conventional content, structure, and purpose.

Google Drive
A cloud file-storage platform. Accepts all file types.

Google Docs, Sheets, Slides, Forms, and Sites
Google's cloud-based documents, spreadsheets, slide presentations, forms, and websites that support synchronous and asynchronous collaboration.

GLOSSARY

Hypothesis
A preliminary claim you make for the purpose of testing against research.

Increment
A small example of content: a title, a phrase, a few sentences, an image, or heading that meets all project requirements.

Instructor review
The instructor's response to increments or drafts for the purpose of identifying strengths of your work and making suggestions for increasing the value of your work as you continue developing content.

Interdependent writing
Activities in which individuals contribute to complex writing projects that no single person could complete on their own.

Interpretation
Explaining what text, images, or actions mean. Paraphrasing is a common interpretation activity.

Learning objectives
Knowledge and skills that students gain while participating in course activities. In this course, your grades are based on demonstrated achievement in five learning objectives:

1. Critical thinking: objectives for interpreting and evaluating information.
2. Research: objectives for gathering and using information.
3. Genre/structure: objectives for specific content development and organization.
4. Synthesis: objectives for using sources material and arriving at original insights.
5. Review/editing: objectives for meeting professional publishing standards.

GLOSSARY

Productivity measures
Ways of accounting for how much work teams and individuals do in a specific amount of time.

Paragraph styles
Sets of attributes that define the appearance of text: most commonly, typeface, type size, type style, line spacing, and text alignment.

Participation
A measure of how frequently, consistently, and effectively students contribute to the class, to content, and to teamwork.

Project requirements
Attributes of written work and team/teammate performance designed to measure learning outcomes.

1. Critical thinking: requirements for interpreting and evaluating information.
2. Research: requirements for gathering and using information.
3. Genre/structure: requirements for specific content development and organization.
4. Synthesis: requirements for using sources material and arriving at original insights.
5. Review/editing: requirements for meeting professional publishing standards.

Project vision
A master document that describes the value, purpose, and learning objectives of a project.

Purpose
The primary reason for developing content for specific audiences. Authors have a purpose for producing content; readers/viewers have a purpose for consuming content.

GLOSSARY

Research question
A sentence in the form of a question that focuses writers' attention on the pursuit of information and knowledge in order to address a problem of interest to specific people or groups.

Review
The process of reflecting on increments or drafts and writing or talking about how well they have met specific objectives.

Revision
Adding, deleting, or modifying content in order to meet objectives more thoroughly and consistently.

Structured activities
Reliable, repeatable activities designed to support interdependent collaboration.

Task redundancy
Assigning tasks to more than one teammate in order to compare teammate perspectives about the purpose of the tasks.

Teamwork
Pursuing shared goals based on consensus about what to accomplish.

Peer review
Reading, annotating, and discussing achievement in specific terms of requirements for critical thinking, research, genre/structure, synthesis, and review/editing.

Task board
A tool for making ideas, tasks, and productivity visible—typically shows intersections of teammates with specific tasks and the status of each task (To do, In process, or Done).

GLOSSARY

Team charter
A collaboratively written document that captures the team's understanding of the best ways to work together.

Teammate interest/confidence inventory
A tool for learning about teammate experience with writing and how they feel about the five basic course learning objectives.

Writing style
The tone of the writing, often described using terms such as formal, conversational, flowery, abstract, or accessible. Style is influenced by sentence structure and word choice.

Writing to learn
Activities designed for learning about a topic by writing about a topic.

INDEX

cause and effect, 37, 40, 68, 96–97
chunk content, 44
citation formatting, 58, 81
citations, 35, 47–48, 52, 58, 69, 82, 84, 146, 156, 164, 187
clarity and focus, 34, 55, 86
commitment, 5, 7, 143–144, 166
commitments: making, 143–144; meeting, 143
communication abilities, 22
communication skills, 14
counter-arguments, 14, 18, 28, 36
credibility, 14, 18, 54, 67–68, 73, 75, 83, 156, 164, 175
critical thinking, vi, 9, 25, 27–28, 34, 35, 67, 70, 73, 91, 98, 130–131, 172, 196

defining, 123, 124, 147–150, 172, 182
design thinking process, 122, 152, 172
disagreements, 13, 114

editing checklist, 59
empathizing, 123, 132–133, 172
evaluate information, 35, 156
evaluative conclusions, 47, 52, 69, 84, 97

headings (descriptive), 43, 45
human impact, 14, 18, 37, 40, 61, 68, 76–77, 96, 147, 156, 164

human-centered approaches, 119, 122, 147
hypothesis, 14, 18, 23, 32, 38, 47, 61, 77, 82, 96, 98, 143

ideating, 124
information: introductory, 42, 68, 80
interest/confidence inventory, 197

keywords, 33, 55–56, 69, 73, 82, 86

listening, 22, 155

measurable results, 37, 41

negotiation tactics, 14

original conclusions, 47, 51

participation, ix, 70, 105, 123, 156–157, 182
prototyping, 124, 127, 151
research methods, 37, 40, 98

research question, 14, 18, 23, 37–39, 61, 68, 76–77, 82, 96–98, 164
researching, x, 36, 40, 51, 55–56, 77, 129
responsive to others, 13
retrospective meetings, 126, 131

signal phrases, 47, 51, 69, 75, 82–83, 156, 164

INDEX

situational awareness, 14
structuring, vi, 25
synthesizing, vi, 51, 52

team charter, 10, 100, 106, 109, 134–135, 172, 181–182
team meetings, 23, 103, 108, 130, 148, 168, 181
team review meetings, 126, 130

team update meetings, 10, 126
team update memos, 145
testing, 7, 143, 194
tone, 14, 18, 28, 31–32, 34, 55–56, 73, 107, 155, 164, 166, 168, 197
topic sentence claims, 47, 50

writing abilities, 23, 25, 59

www.ingramcontent.com/pod-product-compliance
Lightning Source LLC
Chambersburg PA
CBHW061207230426
43664CB00027B/2938